Sacramento City Library
Sacramento, California   95814

_____

.This book is due on the latest date stamped
on the date card.

A fine will be charged for each day that a
book is kept overtime.

AMERICAN POETRY SINCE 1945

A Critical Survey

AMERICAN POETRY SINCE 1945

A Critical Survey by Stephen Stepanchev

HARPER & ROW, PUBLISHERS · NEW YORK

For Gay Wilson Allen

811.09
S827

ACKNOWLEDGMENTS

"A White Paper" by John Ashbery, from *The Tennis Court Oath*, pub-
lished by Wesleyan University Press, copyright © 1962 by John Ashbery.
Reprinted by permission of Wesleyan University Press. "Anaphora,"
"Arrival at Santos," "At the Fishhouses," "Chemin de Fer," "The Fish,"
"The Man-Moth," "Roosters," "View of the Capitol from The Library of
Congress," "The Wake" and "water-wagon poem" by Elizabeth Bishop,
from *Poems: North and South—a Cold Spring*, published by Houghton
Mifflin Company, copyright © 1955 by Elizabeth Bishop. Reprinted by
permission of Houghton Mifflin Company. "Snowfall in the Afternoon,"
"Summer, 1960, Minnesota" and "Watering the Horse" by Robert Bly,
from *Silence in the Snowy Fields*, published by Wesleyan University
Press, copyright © 1962 by Robert Bly. Reprinted by permission of
Robert Bly. "I Know a Man," "After Lorca" and excerpted lines from
other poems by Robert Creeley, from *For Love*, published by Charles
Scribner's Sons, copyright © 1962 by Robert Creeley. Reprinted by per-
mission of Charles Scribner's Sons. "The Lifeguard" by James Dickey,
from *Drowning with Others*, published by Wesleyan University Press,
copyright © 1961 by James Dickey and originally printed in *The New
Yorker*. Reprinted by permission of Wesleyan University Press. "Life
Comparison" and "Poem" by Alan Dugan, from *Poems*, published by
Yale University Press, copyright © 1961 by Alan Dugan. Reprinted by
permission of Alan Dugan. "The Ballad of the Enamored Mage," "Four
Pictures of the Real Universe," "Nor is the Past Pure," "Often I Am
Permitted to Return to a Meadow" and "The Structure of Rime IV" by
Robert Duncan, from *The Opening of the Field*, published by Grove
Press, Inc., copyright © 1960 by Robert Duncan. Reprinted by permis-
sion of Grove Press, Inc. Two poems by Robert Duncan, from *Letters*,
published by Jargon Press, copyright © 1958 by Robert Duncan. Re-
printed by permission of Robert Duncan. "Treesbank Poems" by Robert
Duncan, from *Heavenly City, Earthly City*, published by Bern Porter
Books, Calif., copyright 1947 by Robert Duncan. Reprinted by permission
of Robert Duncan. "An Old Man's Winter Night" by Robert Frost, from
Complete Poems of Robert Frost, published by Holt, Rinehart and
Winston, Inc., copyright 1916, 1921 by Holt, Rinehart and Winston, Inc.
Copyright 1944 by Robert Frost. Reprinted by permission of Holt, Rine-
hart and Winston, Inc. "For Anybody's Martyr's Song," "The Little
Pony" and "The Maimed Grasshopper Speaks Up" by Jean Garrigue,
from *The Monument Rose*, published by Farrar, Straus and Giroux, Inc.,
copyright 1953 by Jean Garrigue. Reprinted by permission of Jean
Garrigue. *The Ego and The Centaur* by Jean Garrigue, published by

CONTENTS

1. LINES OF DEVELOPMENT   1

2. ROBERT LOWELL   17

3. RANDALL JARRELL   37

4. KARL SHAPIRO   53

5. ELIZABETH BISHOP   69

6. JEAN GARRIGUE   80

7. RICHARD WILBUR   93

8. W. S. MERWIN   107

9. PROJECTIVE VERSE   124

   a. Charles Olson   136

   b. Robert Duncan   145

    c. Robert Creeley   *151*

    d. Denise Levertov   *157*

10. POPULAR POETRY: ALLEN GINSBERG   *166*

11. THE SUBJECTIVE IMAGE   *175*

    a. James Wright   *180*

    b. Robert Bly   *185*

12. OTHER RECENT POETS   *188*

    a. John Ashbery   *188*

    b. James Dickey   *190*

    c. Alan Dugan   *193*

    d. LeRoi Jones   *195*

    e. Louis Simpson   *198*

    f. William Stafford   *201*

    g. May Swenson   *202*

13. OBSERVATIONS   *205*

14. SELECTED BIBLIOGRAPHY   *211*

INDEX   *215*

[1] *LINES OF DEVELOPMENT*

(a)

American poetry of the period since the Second World War is unquestionably brilliant, dynamic, and new in the sense that it yields fresh images of contemporary places, persons, and activities. It stirs the reader into an intense awareness of what it means to be alive in the middle of the twentieth century. It is authentically new, also, in that it chooses to live on the frontiers of language: it suggests, in word choice and metaphor, what the English language is becoming under the stresses and strains of American life. Every generation accumulates a store of verbal fat—the euphemisms of hypocrisy, the clichés of servility and status-seeking, the imprecisions

1

of lazy thinking—which serves to clog the arteries of feeling like cholesterol and dims the mind trying to observe and understand. Poets burn away the corruptions of fat thinking and feeling with exact phrases and fresh metaphors that may strike the reader, at first, as strange and even obscure. In reality they serve an important public function in maintaining the vitality of the language and the morality of the state. As William Carlos Williams put it in a letter to Robert Creeley that was published in *Origin* for Spring, 1951, "To write badly is an offense to the state since the government can never be more than the government of words. If the language is distorted crime flourishes."

As for attitudes toward man, society, and the realms beyond physics, it is clear that the new poets are wary of commitment to any sort of "otherness" except that represented by their art. By and large, they are disengaged. This generalization is offered with hesitation and trepidation, for among contemporary poets one can find Zen Buddhists, Roman Catholics, Marxists, Jungians, Black Muslims, Eisenhower Republicans, Jeffersonian Democrats, and a host of other believers. But it is true that in the years after 1947 American poets swung away from the liberal sentiments and political optimism of the depression decade and the war years—sentiments that were based on nineteenth-century ideas of progress and the perfectibility of man and his institutions—to a recognition of the ambiguities and possibly irremediable nature of the moral condition of man. Many of them dismiss all Rousseauistic, naturalistic, and Marxist views of man as essentially sentimental. They deny that man, in the Eden-like center of his mind, is a prelapsarian Adam, wholly innocent and good, who is coerced into evil by circumstance and by institutions that get out of hand but can be changed by collective action. In a curiously Calvinistic but nontheological sense, they see him as fallen and as responsible for his fall. William Golding's gloomy but popular novel about the savagery of children, *Lord of the Flies*, sets the tone of their concern. They have a keen sense of the humor and pathos of the position of man, of the conflict between his ideals and his actions, between his creative work and the imminence of his death, between his being and the encroachments of the nonlife around him, and this awareness disposes them to poem-making meditation and forgiveness of spirit, not to action.

The wary individualism of the poets permits them to respond without prejudice, preconception, or cant to the processes of American life, which give rise to values that are often found to be dubious or harmful. The ultimate source of value, for most contemporary poets, is neither God (whose death was prematurely announced in 1891 by Nietzsche) nor society, but the imagination. Beauty, order, and morality come from the imagination because it constructs metaphors and makes comparisons and so arrives at hierarchies of value, at what is good, better, and worse. In this worship of the imagination the new poets are much closer, among their immediate ancestors, to Wallace Stevens, for whom the imagination was God, than to T. S. Eliot, who valued metaphysical otherness. But many of them are aware that metaphysical, political, and social disengagement makes for an almost unbearable confrontation of the self and a daily, nagging uncertainty as to the value of the imagination's values.

Individualism is nothing new, of course, in American life and letters. One recalls the antinomianism of Anne Hutchinson, who insisted that she could talk directly with God and that the truth of the voice within her took precedence over all truth of authority, no matter how high. One remembers Thoreau's civil disobedience, Emerson's stress on self-reliance, and Walt Whitman's ecstatic celebrations of what the self sees and becomes as it travels the cycles of birth, death, and resurrection. For all of these exponents of traditional individualism the discovery of the self was also a discovery of other selves, seen as carrying God within them and therefore equally divine.

The fragmentation of the poets, which is, no doubt, part of the fragmentation of modern life in general, has led to a great deal of autobiography and confessional writing. Feeling secure only when dealing with personally tested facts, they render the loneliness and terror of contemporary life with the terseness and immediacy of

a diary record. They permit no veil of "objective cor-
relatives" to hang between them and their readers; they
distrust the "aesthetic distance" and "anonymity" that
were once prized by poets and critics. John Crowe
Ransom, for example, once attacked "Lycidas" for being
imperfectly "anonymous": the man Milton appeared
too conspicuously in it! Now poets prize experience in
all its rawness and directness, allowing it to acquire
meaning and form in the imagination.

The new poet describes not generic man reacting to
a hostile world (as, for example, Kenneth Fearing and
other poets of the 1930's did) but the poet himself reacting to it, and he places himself with such particu-
larity that he avoids all obvious universality. When he
turns to family history, he floods his poem with unique,
identifying details, as Robert Lowell does in his *Life
Studies*. Similar autobiographical material can be found
in the work of W. D. Snodgrass, Robert Creeley, and
Anne Sexton, to name only three. Disregarding "aesthetic distance," the new poet tells his readers about
his operation, his psychoanalysis, and his difficulties
with his wife, parents, children, and employers.

Autobiography sometimes takes the form of travel
poems, poems about the poet as tourist or man on the
road, the poet as displaced person or outsider with the
special vision and judgment of the disengaged man,
the man looking into windows. Of course, the image of
the man on the road has, from medieval times, suggested

life experience to the European reader, and for Americans in the nineteenth century it symbolized the man who rejects his past for the sake of an unencumbered new life as he explores the potentialities of virgin territory. Walt Whitman wrote the key poem of this future-directed, optimistic strain, "Song of the Open Road," with its forward-moving, glad discovery of distances and the amplitude of time. The road image still appears in American letters, but since the Second World War the focus has been neither on the past, with its horrifying history, nor on the future, with its uncertainties, but on the present, the eternal present: the poet examines the minutes, one by one, reacting intensely to their particular content of pleasure, boredom, or pain. Interestingly enough, Jack Kerouac's picaresque novel, *On the Road*, with its hitchhiking exploration of America, is in this vein, and there is a similar foreshortening or narrowing of time in Samuel Beckett's play about two tramps on the road, *Waiting for Godot*. In W. S. Merwin's poem "Air" the new view of the road is made especially vivid and poignant: the speaker is described as "Walking at night between the two deserts," singing.

The passing of minutes makes the fact of continual change obvious, and so the final emphasis in much travel poetry—as in the work of Jean Garrigue and May Swenson—is on the dazzled but lonely self examining change or the effects of change in a foreign environment that quickly takes on the dimensions of home, of

Iowa or California, and points to other and mighty changes to come. The ruins of an amphitheater, the broken fountain, the yellowing statue carry the meaning of the world. Sometimes it is a matter of discovering what resists civilization, or is beyond it. Mutability is a theme charged with emotion for poets, now as in the past.

(b)

The brilliance of American poetry of the 1940's, 1950's, and 1960's has a history.

What is called new or modern American poetry dates back to about 1910, to that decade of extraordinary ferment in the arts when Pablo Picasso and Marcel Duchamp startled America with Cubist painting; when Igor Stravinsky's strong rhythms and shimmering melodies surprised the world of music; when the impresario Diaghilev presented the great dancer Nijinsky in ballets reflecting new trends in painting and music; and when James Joyce and Gertrude Stein made their early experiments in a prose that reproduced the contents of consciousness with a new freedom and exactness. It was the decade when Greenwich Village came into its own as a haven for artists and writers from all over America, and the air was full of manifestoes and controversies. Most importantly for American poetry, it was the decade of the founding of such little magazines as the *Seven Arts, Others,* the *Little Review,* and, especially, *Poetry,* which Harriet Monroe began to publish monthly from Chicago, in 1912, and which quickly became the outlet for such new poets as Ezra Pound, T. S. Eliot, Carl Sandburg, Vachel Lindsay, Wallace Stevens, and Edgar Lee Masters.

It was in this decade that three important literary currents began their course of attraction, repulsion, and combination.

There was, first of all, the active traditionalism of such poets as Edwin Arlington Robinson and Robert Frost, in whom the past was renewed. They worked in the accentual-syllabic metrics of Tennyson, Swinburne, and Browning, but they gave American poetry the sort of new tilt that a strong personality, determined to tell the truth, can achieve even in traditional measures. They certainly gave notable expression to the terror, loneliness, and desperation of some New England lives. One remembers Robinson's "Eros Turannos," in which a proud, rich woman who is married to a handsome but unstable man withdraws into madness and seclusion rather than face the gossip and pity of townspeople who are aware of her husband's infidelities; "Luke Havergal," in which the death of a lover brings about a man's mental disintegration and leads to suicide; and the famous "Richard Cory," which describes a successful, envied gentleman who, for no apparent reason, "one calm summer night,/ Went home and put a bullet through his head." One thinks of Robert Frost's bitter poem "Out, Out—," in which a boy loses his hand in a buzz saw and then loses his life, too, and people react with indifference, turning quickly to their own affairs, "since they/ Were not the one dead." Frost has another moving poem about human insensitivity, "Home Burial," in which a wife discovers her husband's callousness when their first child dies and he buries it with his own hands in the family cemetery and then turns matter-of-factly to other chores on the farm. And in "Desert Places," a poem about loneliness, Frost remarks that he is not disturbed by the spaces between the stars that the astronomers talk about; "I have it in me so much nearer home/ To scare myself with my own desert places." In none of these poems is the poet's sense of twentieth-century realities distorted by his reliance on traditional rhythms; but, of course, both Robinson and Frost were poets of strong voice, of unmistakable individuality.

Then there was the current of free-verse experimentation that had its initial impulse in the example of Walt Whitman and the *vers-libre* writers of France. The most notable of the free-verse practitioners were associated with the Anglo-American movement known as Imagism, although Imagism did not insist upon free verse as the only method of writing poetry. As Richard

Aldington and Amy Lowell proclaimed in the preface to *Some Imagist Poets* (1915), "We fight for it as for a principle of liberty. . . . We do believe that the individuality of a poet may often be better expressed in free verse than in conventional forms." The Imagists also emphasized concentration, exactness, the vocabulary of common speech, absolute freedom in choice of subject, and the value of the image or the concrete particular. They opposed what they considered to be the vague generalities and sonorities of much nineteenth-century English poetry. The English contingent of the short-lived Imagist movement included T. E. Hulme, D. H. Lawrence, and Richard Aldington; the Americans were Ezra Pound, Amy Lowell, H. D., and John Gould Fletcher. They met and argued in London, but word of their work caught the imagination of poets in New York, where there was a parallel development in free-verse experimentation—notably in the early work of Wallace Stevens and William Carlos Williams—and reached Chicago, where Populism joined free verse to produce the work of Carl Sandburg and Edgar Lee Masters.

The third current of the 1910 decade was symbolism, a late variety of Romanticism. Its adherents continually moved beyond objects and the experience of objects into areas of higher and wider meaning; three artichokes were never merely three artichokes. Symbolism received some of its impetus from the work of the French Symbolist poets Mallarmé, Rimbaud, Laforgue, and Valéry, but it quickly moved beyond them in allusiveness, in richness of historical, psychological, mythological, philosophical, and literary reference. The chief names associated with symbolism were T. S. Eliot, Ezra Pound, and Wallace Stevens, among the Americans. William Butler Yeats was, of course, the major representative of the movement in Great Britain. The fact that some of these poets were traditionalists in technique and others experimented in free forms points to the interaction of the three literary currents of the decade. They were not mutually exclusive.

Most of the poets of the 1910 decade, no matter what their literary orientation, shared a commitment to otherness. They believed in the external reality of the world, loved it, and tried to push it along a path suggested by some sort of idealism, either traditional or revolutionary. For example, Carl Sandburg was committed to a mystique of "the people," whom he wanted to move in a vaguely Socialist direction that proved to be the New Deal. (*The People, Yes* was published in 1936.) In contrast, T. S. Eliot was struck by the fragmentation and materialism of twentieth-century society and favored a return to the social and spiritual order that a strong Church represents.

These ties to the world, these commitments, were

loosened in the 1920's, when postwar disillusionment, Spenglerian prophecies of doom, and Freudian explorations of the irrational forces in human behavior led to a limited, relativistic morality of the single life. The decade confirmed the genius of T. S. Eliot, Ezra Pound, Wallace Stevens, and William Carlos Williams, and discovered Marianne Moore, E. E. Cummings, Robinson Jeffers, and Hart Crane. This remarkable group of poets brought American poetry to an eminence it had never reached before; together with such writers as Ernest Hemingway, William Faulkner, and Eugene O'Neill, they produced a body of work unmatched by any other decade since the 1850's, when *Moby-Dick, Walden, The Scarlet Letter,* and *Leaves of Grass* were published. The three currents of traditionalism, free-verse experimentation, and symbolism swept through the decade in sometimes surprising interplay, evident not only in the work of the authors already mentioned but also in that of such poets as Edna St. Vincent Millay, Conrad Aiken, Elinor Wylie, Louise Bogan, Léonie Adams, and two Negro poets, Langston Hughes and Countee Cullen.

In the period from 1930 to 1945, American poetry moved in a leftward, populist, mildly Marxist direction; it carried imagery of strikes, decaying machinery, conspiracy, war, and revolution. Even such symbolist poets as Wallace Stevens—habitually detached from the social scene—made gestures toward involvement, as in the poem entitled "The Men That Are Falling" in *The Man with the Blue Guitar* (1937). The reason for these new social and economic commitments is clear, of course, from the events of the time: the stock-market crash of 1929, the subsequent economic depression that led to large-scale unemployment, and the rise of Fascism in Italy, Germany, and Spain, which cast menacing shadows on the international scene throughout the 1930's and eventually led to the Spanish Civil War and World War II. The best American poets of the new liberal orientation were Archibald MacLeish, Horace Gregory, Kenneth Fearing, and Muriel Rukeyser; they served as national poetic barometers. However, they were overshadowed by their brilliant British counterparts, who enjoyed enormous prestige in American intellectual circles: W. H. Auden, Stephen Spender, C. Day Lewis, and Louis MacNeice. And it should be noted that the new movement generated a right-wing Agrarian opposition in the South which drew the support, in varying degrees, of such tradition-directed poets as Allen Tate, John Crowe Ransom, and Robert Penn Warren.

Technically, the poetry of 1930–1945 reflected the three movements of traditionalism, symbolism, and free-form composition. Symbolism was very strong, and it is one of the curious paradoxes of the period that poems about the plight of underpaid workers, sharecroppers, and the unemployed were made of symbols and elliptical, allusive phrases that few workers were willing to puzzle out.

(c)

In the early months of 1945 (from February 28 to April 25), Muriel Rukeyser conducted a poetry workshop at the California Labor School in San Francisco. Later in the same year Karl Shapiro won a Pulitzer Prize for his book of war poems, *V-Letter and Other Poems*. By the end of the year two substantial collections of war poems were published: *The War Poets*, edited by the influential anthologist Oscar Williams, and *War and the Poet*, edited by Richard Eberhart and Selden Rodman. Taken together, these facts point to the "engagement" of American poets during the war years, their interest in economics, politics, and public events, partly, perhaps, as a carry-over from commitments during the depression decade. But within eight years, by the end of the Korean War in 1953, the poetry of public issues was completely in disfavor. It was regarded as rhetorical and superficial. It was no longer "hip" to believe in social, political, or economic salvation, and many poets eagerly shed the political labels they had acquired in earlier years. The characteristic poems of the year 1953 were psychological, archetypal, and mythological, like those of Richard Wilbur, W. S. Merwin, and Randall Jarrell.

These poets enjoyed writing rich, complex poems on themes with universal reverberations. They were responsive to the "new criticism" of John Crowe Ransom, Robert Penn Warren, and Cleanth Brooks, the subtlest explicatory criticism in American literary history, which nudged poetic practice in the direction of strongly structured, traditional poetry that reflected not only the systole-diastole of the heart but the ironies and paradoxes of the mind as well.

After 1953 three new trends became evident. The first of these involved a rejection of mythological and psychological archetypes in favor of autobiography and family history: descriptions of parents, grandparents, and uncles; memoirs of a stay in jail, the troubles of marriage, and experiences in a hospital. Illustrative of this trend are such books as *Life Studies*, by Robert Lowell; *Heart's Needle*, by W. D. Snodgrass; and *All My Pretty Ones*, by Anne Sexton. The second movement was largely technical in nature; its adherents opposed the "closed" metrical systems of tradition and championed the free forms of Field Composition or Projective Verse, which was intended to reflect the rhythms of contemporary American speech. The chief spokesman of this movement was Charles Olson, and the best poets associated with it were Denise Levertov, Robert Creeley, and Robert Duncan. The third and most recent movement put emphasis on the "subjective image," that is, the image that arises from the unconscious of the poet and generates powerful emotions beyond the reach of logic or analysis. Two of the ablest poets in this movement were James Wright and Robert Bly.

[2] *ROBERT LOWELL*

Of the poets who came into public notice in the years immediately after World War II, Robert Lowell has the most inclusive vision, encompassing both the terrors of responsibility and the terrors of alienation, and his career reflects most clearly two major trends in recent American poetry. These are the shift from "otherness" to the metaphysics and ethics of the individual imagination and the abandonment of the strict measures and dense phrasing of symbolist verse for the looser measures and simpler diction of a poetry responsive to the breath and cadence of contemporary reality.

It is a remarkable fact that, during his brief stay at Harvard University, Mr. Lowell wrote free verse in the manner of William Carlos Williams; however, none of it was published. He developed his strong first style, with its Christian symbolism and intricate formalism, when he transferred to Kenyon College and came under the influence of John Crowe Ransom, then an important exponent of the "new criticism" and author of graceful, elegiac verses on the death of fair women, families, and the chivalric tradition. Mr. Lowell achieved his first publication as a poet in the Winter, 1939, issue of the *Kenyon Review*, edited by Ransom, but it was not until the Cummington Press issued his first book of poems, *Land of Unlikeness*, in 1944, that his quality as a poet became evident. This work was partly in debt to Allen Tate, a Southern Agrarian and classicist, with whom Lowell lived and worked for a year, but its pervasive Roman Catholicism should not be attributed to the influence of Tate, since Lowell's conversion from New England Calvinism (or, rather, the reminders of the tradition) preceded Tate's own turn to Rome.

Clearly, the "otherness" of Robert Lowell was not the same as that of the poets with commitments to Marxism or New Deal liberalism or some undefined popular democracy. It was related to the neo-Thomism of the universities (where, in the 1930's, attempts were made to synthesize Marxism and Roman Catholicism), to T. S. Eliot's view of the importance of a Church as the focal center of a culture, and to the religious orthodoxy expressed in Ransom's *God without Thunder*. That this position was held by a minority of poets in the war year 1944 is clear from the acidity of Allen Tate's remarks about democratic poets in his introduction to *Land of Unlikeness:* "The history of poetry shows that good verse does not inevitably make its way; but unless, after the war, the small public for poetry shall exclude all except democratic poets who enthusiastically greet the advent of the slave-society, Robert Lowell will have to be reckoned with."

The war moved Lowell profoundly; he spent part of it in prison as a conscientious objector, refusing to share responsibility for the bombing of cities. Roman Catholicism gave him the symbols and prayers with which to understand and exorcise the horrors of the war and man's ancient cruelty to man. Although these symbols were unfashionable in 1944, they were present, inert, in the consciousness of all readers of poetry—Catholics, Protestants, and Jews alike. Lowell's passion revitalized them. He emerged as a national or "people's" poet, like T. S. Eliot, because of his brooding concern for the spiritual condition and destiny of his country-men.

In his bitter war poem "On the Eve of the Feast of the Immaculate Conception, 1942," Lowell attacks the cannibalism and spiritual blindness of Christians who invoke the Virgin's aid to "improve/ On the big wars." In "The Bomber" he ironically addresses an airman in these terms:

O godly bomber, and most
A god when cascading tons
Baptized the infidel Huns
For the Holy Ghost,
Did you know the name of flight
When you blasted the bloody sweat
And made the noonday night:
When God and Satan met
And Christ gave up the ghost?

The diction of this stanza is strained, notably in the clause "When you blasted the bloody sweat," but the tension of contraries in the "godly bomber" and in the meeting of God and Satan strongly conveys Lowell's feeling that Christ dies again and again in the air raids of the war. In "Christmas Eve in the Time of War: A Capitalist Meditates by a Civil War Monument," a rich man broods about "the venery of capital" and the death of his son in battle, even as he celebrates the birth of Christ: "But woe unto the rich that are with child."

The other major theme of *Land of Unlikeness* is historical; Lowell contrasts the past with the present, sometimes to show how the grandeur and idealism of early America have declined into the materialism and spiritual disrepair of the present and, in other poems, to trace out the historical roots of the crimes and guilts of contemporary man. For example, in "The Park Street Cemetery" Lowell asks, "What are Sam Adams and

Cotton Mather?" In his sonnet "Salem" he describes "seasick spindrift" and "oily slick" and sewage that "sickens the rebellious seas" and longs for the heroism of the past: "Where was it that New England bred the men/ Who quartered the Leviathan's fat flanks/ And fought the British Lion to his knees?" But Lowell's ambivalence toward New England history is amply evident in such lines as these from "Children of Light": "Our fathers wrung their bread from stocks and stones/ And fenced their gardens with the Redman's bones." In his sonnet "Concord" he speaks of Mammon's "unbridled industry" in twentieth-century America, but he also invokes images of an unromantic past: "The death-dance of King Philip and his scream/ Whose echo girdled this imperfect globe."

Lowell's ambivalent attitude toward history (evident also in such poems as "Dea Roma," which touches on the glory and bloodguilt of Rome) suggests T. S. Eliot's position in *The Waste Land*, where the magnificence of the spiritual triumphs of the past is contrasted with the soulless materialism of the present, but where, also, the source of contemporary spiritual ills is traced back to the fragmentation of the Renaissance. Eliot seems to have influenced Lowell even in the choice of title, *Land of Unlikeness*, though the source of the phrase itself is St. Bernard. The elegiac tone of the book is clearly Eliotic, but it also has some relationship to the tone of Southern poets mourning the death of the Confederacy, as in Tate's "Ode to the Confederate Dead" and in Ransom's poem "Old Mansion."

Technically, *Land of Unlikeness* is a very competent performance. The poet counts his accents and syllables and arranges them carefully in iambic measure, in three-foot, four-foot, and five-foot lengths, varying from the iambs frequently in order to avoid monotony and to achieve emphasis. He organizes his verse in complex stanzaic patterns and rhyme schemes that engage the mind, ear, and eye (some of the poems were first written in blank verse and then adapted to rhymed stanzas). As Allen Tate remarked in 1944, "There is no other poetry today quite like this. T. S. Eliot's recent prediction that we should soon see a return to formal and even intricate meters and stanzas was coming true, before he made it, in the verse of Robert Lowell." But what Allen Tate did not say is that the book is the work of a poet of still uncertain taste, with a predilection for staged contrasts, violent diction, strained figures of speech, bombast, and melodrama.

By the time Lowell published his second book, *Lord Weary's Castle*, in 1946, the awkwardness and exaggeration were much less evident. He had developed his fine first manner and was writing poems of a high specific gravity, so dense that every square inch had its image, allusion, or textured phrase. Many of the poems in *Land of Unlikeness* were drastically revised for reprinting in the new book. For example, "Christmas Eve in the Time of War: A Capitalist Meditates by a Civil War Monument" lost its capitalist brooding over his son, killed in battle, and the title became, simply, "Christmas Eve Under Hooker's Statue."

In *Lord Weary's Castle*, Lowell continues his despairing, prophet-like studies of the contemporary wasteland; the Lord Weary of the title is everyman, and his castle, now in ruins, has been built by the good mason Christ, who has received no payment for his work. Lowell implies that recognition of the value of this work would revitalize Lord Weary. The religious theme is intertwined with the historical theme in such poems as "The Dead in Europe" and "At the Indian Killer's Grave," in which the New England past is presented under this barbed epigraph from "The Gray Champion" by Nathaniel Hawthorne: "Here, also, are the veterans of King Philip's War, who burned villages and slaughtered young and old, with pious fierceness, while the godly souls throughout the land were helping them with prayer." (This poem appeared, in a different version, in *Land of Unlikeness* under the title "The Park Street Cemetery.") But the book also contains a number of translations or adaptations from Rimbaud, Valéry, Rilke, and Sextus Propertius, which represent Lowell's attempt to see the world through the eyes and technique of other poets, a useful exercise in sympathy. And some have a distinctly autobiographical character, like "In the Cage," or take their impulse from family history, as in the elegies "The Quaker Graveyard in Nantucket" and "In Memory of Arthur Winslow."

Several of the poems represent high achievements in the first Lowell manner (only a few are reworkings of poems that first appeared in *Land of Unlikeness*), among them "Colloquy in Black Rock," "Christmas Eve Under Hooker's Statue," "Mary Winslow," "Salem," "Concord," "Children of Light," "The Drunken Fisherman," "Napoleon Crosses the Berezina," "As a Plane Tree by the Water," "The Ghost," "After the Surprising Conversions," and, especially, "The Quaker Graveyard in Nantucket," which was written in memory of Warren Winslow, a cousin who, together with his comrades aboard a Navy ship, had been lost at sea in World War II. This elegy is the finest poem in *Lord Weary's Castle*, both because of its technical brilliance—its careful shifts in rhythm, its compact imagery, its appropriate modulations of tone—and because of its moving treatment of basic questions about the moral nature of man and his relationship to God, questions that embarrass many poets into silence, fearing cliché and failure.

Three ideas recur in the poem and animate it, stirring the poet and his reader into meditation and feeling: the precariousness of human life and the whole God-begun evolutionary process; the stupidity of greed and murder (as in the case of the fighting Quakers of

Nantucket) in any metaphysical context; and the inscrutability of God, who encompasses all the contraries and ambivalences of reality, very much like Herman Melville's White Whale.

The poem begins with an epigraph from the Bible —"Let man have dominion over the fishes of the sea and the fowls of the air and the beasts and the whole earth and every creeping creature that moveth upon the earth"—which must be read again at the end of the poem for its irony. The work is divided into seven parts. In the first section a member of the crew of a battleship in the North Atlantic Fleet describes, in vivid detail, the corpse of a drowned sailor who is dragged up from the sea and then returned to it, weighted, with eyes closed. In parts II, III, IV, and V the scene is the Quaker graveyard in Nantucket, and the speaker, presumably the poet, addresses his drowned cousin, meditating on the power of water to destroy life and on the drive of the Ahabs of the world to kill beast, man, God, or whatever stands in the way of the fulfillment of their greedy, mad ambitions. The horror and corruption of their lives are symbolized, in section V, by the whale's viscera, seen as overrunning the world and bringing on the fires of the Day of Judgment, when only the mercy of Christ can save mankind. In part VI the scene shifts to Walsingham, England, to an old shrine where the speaker, a pilgrim, sees a statue of the Virgin and discovers that her "expressionless" face "expresses God": she knows what God knows; she is beyond birth, suffering, and death. Coming after the heave and horror and gore of the preceding sections of the poem, the Walsingham sequence represents an interval of calm when water appears life-giving; but the vision of God with which it closes is terrifying in its dreamless mysticism. The concluding section of the poem returns the reader to the meditative poet at the cenotaph in the Quaker grave-yard; here he recognizes and accepts the fact that God gives life and takes it away: "The Lord survives the rainbow of His will." And here he sees the death of his sailor cousin in a context so vast that individual sorrow seems pointless and possibly blasphemous.

The basic measure of this remarkable poem is iambic pentameter, but the poet veers into trimeter and tetrameter as the sense, movement, and mood of the poem require. He is especially careful to vary from iambic measure when he wishes to suggest violent storm action or harpooners hacking at a whale. Consider the opening lines:

A brackish reach of shoal off Madaket,—
The sea was still breaking violently and night
Had steamed into our North Atlantic Fleet . . .

The first and third lines are in iambic pentameter, with-out variation, but the second and fourth feet of the second line are anapaests that break the rhythm to suggest the movement of the sea. Or take these lines from section V:

> The death-lance churns into the sanctuary, tears
> The gun-blue swingle, heaving like a flail,
> And hacks the coiling life out: it works and drags . . .

The first line is in iambic hexameter, and the second foot is a spondee; the second line is in iambic pentameter, but the second foot is a spondee; and the third line is regular except for the third foot, which is an amphibrach. All these variations assist in creating the barbaric excitement of the whale-kill.

The effectiveness of these passages is due, in part, to such strong verbs as "was breaking," "steamed," "churns," "tears," "hacks," "works," and "drags" and to the vivid, concentrated imagery which these verbs help to create—of the sea breaking, the night steaming, and the death-lance churning "into the sanctuary." The poet dramatically alters the tone of his imagery as the poem moves from the violence of the whale-hunt to the peace of the Walsingham countryside, with its "small trees" and "munching English lane." In part III he moves from an image of Quakers drowning "in the sperm-whale's slick" to their ironic, wrongheaded insistence that God is on their side.

Lowell's third book of poems, *The Mills of the Kavanaughs*, which appeared in 1951, represents the end of a phase, a style, a commitment. As in *Lord Weary's Castle*, Christian symbolism is dominant, but now it is heavily reinforced by allusions to Greek mythology and the Latin classics. The verse is still under tight formal control—carefully structured and measured, chiefly in iambic pentameter. The title poem, for example, is in rhymed iambic pentameter couplets which are grouped in sixteen-line stanzas. The elegiac strain of *Lord Weary's Castle* is still present; of the seven poems in the book five are about death, decline, or madness. "Mother Marie Therese (Drowned in 1912)" is a soliloquy spoken by a Canadian nun as she recalls with affection a lively sister whom a priest characterized as "An émigrée in this world and the next." "Falling Asleep Over the Aeneid" focuses on an ineffectual old man in Concord who falls asleep while reading the *Aeneid* and so fails to attend Sunday morning service. While asleep, he dreams that he is Aeneas at the funeral of his comrade Pallas, and, on awaking, he recalls the death of his Uncle Charles, who was a commander of colored troops in the Civil War. These memories suggest a contrast between the state-making idealism of the past and the dusty bookishness of the present. But the most ambitious poem in the collection is "The Mills of the Kavanaughs," which is a long narrative poem about the decline of a rich and powerful Maine family. The story is told from the point of view of Anne, a poor girl from a family of thirteen children, who is first adopted by the Kavanaughs and then married to the son, Harry, the last of the family line, in the hope that she will bring life to it. Her husband is called up by the Navy just before the Pearl Harbor disaster; when he returns home, insane, he tries to strangle her in bed one night because she speaks aloud, in a dream, to a man who he supposes is her lover. Shortly thereafter he dies, and Anne becomes, indeed, the queen of the dead in the Kavanaugh garden. The pathos of her position is rendered in magnificent imagery and powerful memory sequences that show the ambivalence of her attitude toward her husband and his heritage of success and failure. But the poem suffers from an artificial, imposed symbolism that calls attention to itself. For example, Anne plays solitaire in her garden with the Douay Bible as her imaginary opponent, Sol, to suggest that she is in Hades. Her husband's grave is in the garden, and she thinks of it as a "buried bed." Near a millpond rises a statue of Persephone, to emphasize the parallel between the kingdom of Dis and the land of the Kavanaughs, where the life-giving attributes of Persephone are inoperative.

When Lowell published his next book, *Life Studies*, in 1959, readers were immediately struck by a remarkable change in subject matter, style, and philosophy. For one thing, the poet had lost his allegiance to the otherness represented by the doctrines and symbolism of the Roman Catholic Church and had moved to a morality that the self pieces together from experience or evaluations of experience. That this morality was not vastly different from the morality of the Church is obvious from the poems, in which Lowell is still very much concerned about the social order and its decay. As he remarked to Frederick Seidel in an interview for the *Paris Review*, "The morality seems much the same. But the symbolism is gone; you couldn't possibly say what creed I believed in." The key poem, signaling the change, is "Beyond the Alps," first published in 1953, in which Lowell speaks of the dogma of Mary's bodily assumption into heaven, enunciated in 1950 by Pius XII, in these terms:

> The lights of science couldn't hold a candle
> to Mary risen—at one miraculous stroke,
> angel-wing'd, gorgeous as a jungle bird!
> But who believed this? Who could understand?

Much of the Christian symbolism and most of the extrinsic classical symbolism of *The Mills of the Kavanaughs* are now gone; Lowell's stress on experience as experience parallels the practice of such anti-symbolists as Kenneth Rexroth. He brings into his poetry more and more of the prosaic, seemingly intractable materials of ordinary American reality, and, in particular, the facts of his own life and his family's history. It is in the confessional intimacies of autobiography that Lowell now finds release from the restrictions that the "new critics" had imposed upon him, and what symbolism remains in the poems—poetry, after all, cannot exist without symbols—is intrinsic and so subtle that the reader is not offended by the need to make continual equations.

The new Lowell manner suits the new confessional matter admirably. The poet loosens the tight metrical structures to which he had been partial and allows for conversational cadences. Speaking of his earlier style to Frederick Seidel, he said: "I thought it was getting increasingly stifling. I couldn't get my experience into tight metrical forms." Here, as an example of the new style, is the concluding stanza of "Skunk Hour," one of the best poems in the book, a terrifying vision of social decay, in which everyone in a small resort town in Maine is seen as a skunk-like parasite and scavenger, including the "I" character, who as artist and voyeur lives on what he sees—love-cars and tombs in congruence—and is unsure whether he or his world is insane:

I stand on top
of our back steps and breathe the rich air—
a mother skunk with her column of kittens swills the
garbage pail.
She jabs her wedge-head in a cup
of sour cream, drops her ostrich tail,
and will not scare.

This stanza, like the rest of the poem, sounds like free verse—it seems so unhampered in its easy rise and fall —but, actually, it can be scanned, and one hears rhymes. The words "top" and "cup" are off-rhymes, to be sure, but "air" and "scare" and "pail" and "tail" rhyme perfectly. The first and sixth lines are in iambic dimeter; the second, fourth, and fifth are in iambic tetrameter; and the third line is in iambic heptameter. It seems clear that, while aiming at freedom, Lowell could not throw off the discipline and craft of his early training or reject the pleasures of traditional form.

Life Studies contains transitional poems like "Beyond the Alps"; an autobiographical prose work entitled "91 Revere Street," which is a witty, unsentimental report on the poet's childhood in Boston; poetic portraits of Ford Madox Ford, Hart Crane, and George Santayana; and poems about his grandparents, parents, the tensions of marriage, a stay in a mental hospital, and an experience in prison as a conscientious objector.

In addition to "Skunk Hour" and "Beyond the Alps," the notable poems of the book are "Waking in the Blue," "Memories of West Street and Lepke," and "Man and Wife." In these poems carefully selected details add up to a moving recovery of experience; they have weight and power. In some of the other autobiographical poems, however, the perceptions, although striking in themselves, seem inconsequential.

Lowell's next book appeared in 1962; it was a collection of translations from various European poets, a veritable anthology of great poetry by Homer, Sappho, Villon, Leopardi, Baudelaire, Rilke, Montale, Pasternak, and others. The book was called *Imitations* because of the poet's many departures from the original texts in search of an "alive English" that the authors would have used "if they were writing their poems now and in America." Lowell worked from original versions in languages that he knew, but he buttressed his knowledge with translations by other poets, to whose work he refers rather ungratefully in these terms: "Swarms of published translations were useful and irritating to me." In the case of Pasternak, he worked from prose translations supplied him by "Russian readers," a most unsatisfactory procedure, as he composed without any sense of the rhythms and connotations of the Russian language. These "imitations" were done when the poet was unable to do anything of his own, but they do not represent departures from former practice, since such imitations had appeared in previous books: adaptations of Sextus Propertius, Rilke, Rimbaud, and Valéry.

The collection is certainly readable and "alive" in language, and a few of the poems have the technical rightness of original poems, notably the section called "Heine Dying in Paris," Baudelaire's "The Ruined Garden," Rilke's "The Cadet Picture of My Father," and Montale's "The Chess Player." Lowell is weakest in his translations from Pasternak and Rimbaud, particularly in the case of "The Drunken Boat," which he has reduced by a third and stripped of most of its complex, magical imagery.

Imitations did not enhance Lowell's position as a poet, but by the middle 1960's it was nevertheless clear that he had successfully crossed the rapids and floods of postwar American poetry and had emerged as a poet of national scope with a flexible style capable of rendering contemporary life.

His most recent book, *For the Union Dead* (1964), contains many poems in the confessional and autobiographical mode that characterized *Life Studies*, notably "The Old Flame," in which the poet focuses on memories of an unhappy marriage. The speaker and his wife are said to be "quivering and fierce" as they lie "In one bed and apart." In another poem, "Middle Age," Lowell sees himself as aging in New York, a city that "drills" through his nerves, and he recalls his father at his age, who left "dinosaur/ death-steps on the crust,/ where I must walk." He asks his father to forgive him his injuries, "as I forgive/ those I/ have injured!" Clearly, this is a Lowell of impressive psychological and moral penetration. But the most interesting feature of the new work is Lowell's return to the vatic utterance of *Land of Unlikeness* and *Lord Weary's Castle*. The best poem in the book, the title poem, reveals the poet's overwhelming concern for the destiny of the American people and of mankind in general. Ostensibly about a Civil War

monument in Boston showing Colonel Shaw leading a
Negro regiment into battle, half of whom were killed,
the poem examines human progress, as represented by
a new underground garage being built on the site of
the old Boston Aquarium, on the one hand, and by the
new weaponry of the atomic age, on the other. Lowell
observes, with despair, that the "ditch" and "space"
are nearer than they were in the years of the Civil War,
for people are dedicated to selfish personal ends and
are indifferent to larger questions of social and international well-being. The Aquarium, he says, is gone, and

> Everywhere
> giant finned cars nose forward like fish;
> a savage servility
> slides by on grease.

This is a strong indictment of the contemporary
world, built of an awareness of American history and of
the passing of time. Like T. S. Eliot, Lowell has a historical imagination; the past is wholly alive for him and
helps to clarify the present. It is out of this awareness
that Lowell has been moved to write a two-part play,
The Old Glory, which the American Place Theatre
produced in New York in the fall of 1964. This work
is a dramatization of "My Kinsman, Major Molineux,"
by Nathaniel Hawthorne, and of "Benito Cereno," by
Herman Melville. The two stories have this in common:

they both describe a corrupt society (a town in New England in the first story and a ship full of mutinous slaves in the other) which imposes upon and tries to destroy the good, the just, and the innocent. It is obvious that in his return to social themes, after a period of writing highly personal poetry, Lowell is making a savage attack on society, as savage as that of Friedrich Dürrenmatt in *The Visit* and yet as full of love as the tirades of the prophets of the Old Testament.

[3] *RANDALL JARRELL*

Like his friend Robert Lowell, Randall Jarrell came into prominence as a poet in a time of economic troubles, Fascism, war, and revolution. Even as far back as 1936 he received the encouragement of a prize in poetry from the *Southern Review*, which was one of the influential literary quarterlies of the depression decade. In 1940, New Directions published a group of his poems in *Five Young American Poets*, First Series; and in the grim war year 1942, Harcourt, Brace, and Company issued his first collection of poems, *Blood for a Stranger*. The very title of this book pointed to crisis and the sort

37

of generosity that a society discovers it is capable of
feeling in a time of general peril.

Reflecting on the crimes, terrors, and guilts of a
period that W. H. Auden once characterized as low and
dishonest, Jarrell's poems suggest the pain and in-
credulity of a child discovering the hypocritical ways
of adults. One finds images of rejection, social disrup-
tion, flight, and transformation, as in the poem "For an
Emigrant," which describes a Viennese who fled first to
Prague and then to America before "The Accuser, the
Appeaser, the inhuman Judge." The poem ends with
this wholesale indictment: "Because of us, because of
what we did or did not do,/ See, the men die." Another
poem on the theme of flight is "The Refugees," a brilliantly conceived work in which displaced persons are
pictured as traveling on a train that suddenly assumes a
metaphysical character:

> What else are the lives but a journey to the vacant
>   Satisfaction of death? And the mask
>   They wear tonight through their waste
> Is death's rehearsal. *For I too shall escape,*
>   We read in the faces; and what is there we possessed
>   That we were unwilling to trade for this?

All journeys have this fatefulness for Jarrell; in "On
the Railway Platform" he remarks, "Turn where you
may,/ You travel by the world's one way," and then

adds, "journeys end in/ No destination we meant." It is this emphasis on motion, on man as forever changing even as the landscape through which he travels changes its configuration of mountains, plains, and rivers, that characterizes Jarrell's essentially science-conditioned view of reality. The end of motion is a rest or a death as the cycle renews.

The imagery of war and revolution and the bloody changes they produce is central to many of the poems in *Blood for a Stranger*. The destruction of the Spanish Republic in the fires of civil war aroused the indignation of many poets in the 1930's; Jarrell was moved to write two poems on the subject, "For the Madrid Road" and "A Poem for Someone Killed in Spain." In a poem entitled "1789–1939" he deals with revolutions and counterrevolutions in a historical perspective stretching back to the French Revolution; he comments despairingly on the horrors and betrayals of European history. In an ambitious poem entitled "The Winter's Tale," he examines this history with an Eliot-*cum*-Spengler gloom, taking the position that only disaster can result from the misuse of intelligence and knowledge for the perfection of war technology:

> From the disintegrating bomber, the mercenary
> Who has sown without hatred or understanding
> The shells of the absolute world that flowers
> In the confused air of the dying city

> Plunges for his instant of incandescence, acquiesces
> In our death and his own, and welcomes
> The fall of the western hegemonies.

The poem has the bitterness of Picasso's mural about the bombing of Guernica.

Some of these poems are written from the point of view of a child, a convenient symbol of innocence for Jarrell as for Blake, of what each man imagines himself to be in the secret center of his being, no matter how old he is, for there he can always resist the coercions of circumstance, the agonies and corruptions of experience. In reality, of course, he can't. Jarrell feels pity for the child who inevitably becomes an adult by suffering the blows of time and by assuming the guilt of his desires. This preoccupation with childhood is perhaps astonishing in the case of the least naïve of all contemporary poets. Jarrell's sophistication, wit, and quickness of mind are extraordinary, and yet, again and again, he returns to the theme of babes lost in a dark wood, as in the poem "Fear," in which he describes the betrayal of children by "That dreaming and inhuman world,/ The forest of a winter night." Fairy-tale characters like Jack of beanstalk fame populate the poems. No doubt Jarrell sees these figures as archetypes of human experience, as revelations like those of Freudian and Jungian psychology, but they lack the deep, obsessional power of the images in Robert Lowell's poetry.

They are tamed by the consciousness of the poet; they have the surface persuasion of something lighted by the mind. For the poet of unusual intelligence sentiment often substitutes for passion.

Sentiment is appropriate, of course, to a poetry of public issues, as the example of W. H. Auden, the great literary influence of the 1930's and 1940's, makes clear. Jarrell learned from him how to describe the contemporary world, how to join the processes of the heart and the mind. He learned to work in a modern idiom that absorbed the abstractions of politics, history, and the developing sciences of psychology and sociology. But it should not be assumed, because of his technical association with the school of Auden, that Jarrell was a Marxist. He shared with the Marxists some of their sympathies and antipathies—as in the case of Spain and Fascism—but he was too freewheeling an intellectual to be bound by any program. Born in Nashville, educated at Vanderbilt University, and employed, at various times, by Kenyon College, the University of Texas, and the Woman's College of the University of North Carolina, he was under the counterinfluence of conservative, tradition-directed Southern opinion. Quick to see incongruities and complexities, he has always moved unhampered wherever his imagination and feelings directed.

Jarrell spent four years (1942–1946) in the United States Army Air Force, part of the time as celestial-navigation tower operator at a base for B-29 aircraft in Arizona. During those years he collected the images of war action and inaction that give substance to two books, *Little Friend, Little Friend* (1945) and *Losses* (1948). Reading them, one senses at once the vigor of an artist who has found his "matter." Jarrell's imagination and wit pounce upon Army routines, armor, strategies, and engagements and make them yield symbolic experience. His war poems have a powerful urgency and clarity; he is obviously eager to have his reader *see:* he is not afraid of the sort of direct statement that he avoided in his first book, where so often an obscurity takes the place of illumination in the conclusions of poems. And the war details sound authentic, unlike those in *Blood for a Stranger*, which were merely illustrative of principles and attitudes. As Henry James once remarked, it is possible for a young lady from the provinces to write about garrison life if she has a lively imagination, but she would do better to work from familiar premises.

Little Friend, Little Friend is a strong book, clear in outline and detail: it produces a sharp impression of the realities of war from the point of view of the soldier. He is shown saying goodbye to freedom at a port of embarkation. Resentful of a world that makes his life a number and a commodity, he wants to hear his name called, to assert his identity, as in the poem "Mail Call." But in "The Difficult Resolution" Jarrell makes this soldierly comment:

> Remember what you learned then: that you are
>   powerless
> Except to know that you are powerless, to learn
> Your use and your rejection, all that is destroying you—
> And to accept it: the difficult resolution.

This sort of acceptance means, ultimately, an acceptance of death, the transformer, as in the poem "The Metamorphoses," in which a man dies in an explosion on a wharf where bombers are crated. Clearly, Jarrell is still fascinated by change, by the cycles of reality, as he is by childhood, by the special conscience of innocence, for again and again in these poems one finds the soldier compared to a child. One of the best is "Absent with Official Leave," in which a soldier is shown escaping the horrors of the world by going to sleep like a child and then awaking in the morning to the possibility of death. Another bitter, powerful poem, "The Death of the Ball Turret Gunner," produces an effective contrast between images of birth and details of war action in the sky:

> From my mother's sleep I fell into the State,
> And I hunched in its belly till my wet fur froze.
> Six miles from earth, loosed from its dream of life,
> I woke to black flak and the nightmare fighters.
> When I died they washed me out of the turret with a
>   hose.

In *Losses*, Jarrell continues his examination of

military life in such poems as "The Dead Wingman,"
"Pilots, Man Your Planes," "The Dead in Melanesia,"
and "The Subway from New Britain to the Bronx." As
might be expected, he touches on the themes of innocence and change. And here he develops a new area of
concern, the massacre of the Jews in the camps of Nazi
Germany, reports of which had shocked the world in
the early postwar years. In two poems, "A Camp in the
Prussian Forest" and "Jews at Haifa," he comments on
the horror of the Jewish experience of the roads of the
world; in the latter poem a refugee looks at the prom-
ised land and speaks movingly of wisdom and hope:

> There is no hope; "in all this world
> There is no other wisdom
> Than ours: we have understood the world,"
> We think; but hope, in dread
> Search for one doubt, and whisper: "Truly, we are
>   not dead."

The ease with which human beings can withhold
empathy from those they consider their enemies is one
of the bitterest aspects of this wisdom. Hearing about
atrocities, they can go on watering their flowers or playing with their cats and dogs. It is this sort of discovery
that is at the heart of a poem entitled "Eighth Air
Force":

> If, in an odd angle of the hutment,
> A puppy laps the water from a can

Of flowers, and the drunk sergeant shaving
Whistles *O Paradiso!*—shall I say that man
Is not as men have said: a wolf to man?

The other murderers troop in yawning;
Three of them play Pitch, one sleeps, and one
Lies counting missions, lies there sweating
Till even his heart beats: One; One; One.
O murderers! . . . Still, this is how it's done:

This is a war. . . . But since these play, before they
        die,
Like puppies with their puppy; since, a man,
I did as these have done, but did not die—
I will content the people as I can
And give up these to them: Behold the man!

I have suffered, in a dream, because of him,
Many things; for this last saviour, man,
I have lied as I lie now. But what is lying?
Men wash their hands, in blood, as best they can:
I find no fault in this just man.

Jarrell sees the moral complexity of the human condition, but perhaps, in view of the genocidal potential
of atomic weapons, he is too easily reconciled to man's
capacity for evil. The last two lines of the poem imply
an acceptance of "just" bloodshed.

The poem illustrates features of Jarrell's writing
technique. There is, first of all, the dramatic, first-
person account of life in an Air Force hutment, with
carefully selected details to give the reader a sense of be-

ing there. There is the strong contrast between the tender care represented by the puppy lapping water from "a can/ Of flowers" and the death-dealing mission from which the airmen have returned: they now yawn, sleep, shave, play Pitch, or count missions. The "I" character identifies with the airmen in order not to appear an outsider, judging without comprehension. He entertains contrasting ideas: murder and salvation, playing and dying, guilt and innocence, lying and telling the truth, soiling one's hands and washing them, justice and injustice. He comes to a resolution in the paradoxical line: "Men wash their hands, in blood, as best they can."

The conversational verse line is characteristic of Jarrell, but he likes to work in a traditional measure—in this case iambic pentameter. He subjects it to as many variations as possible, to see how far he can go without actually abandoning it. It is as though he were afraid that someone might suspect him of counting accents and syllables. The effect is loose, colloquial, "sprung." But he does not give up rhymes, which are the nails of his structure and make for emphasis. He returns again and again to the crucial words "can" and "man."

Jarrell's fourth book of poems, *The Seven-League Crutches*, appeared in 1951. It represented a notable decline in intensity and involvement, for the poet could no longer work in the galvanizing "otherness" of themes relating to public peril; he had to settle for the minor crises of personal, peacetime life. The journey motif is still present, as the title suggests, but the metaphysics is muted; one sees a tourist in Austria, examining an English garden. The theme of innocence persists in poems about children bemused by illness, dream, and myths of transformation. One poem is about a girl asleep, waiting to be awakened; another is about a girl in a library, reading her life away. The poems are relaxed, garrulous, pleasant; they lack urgency. Among the best are "The Black Swan," on the theme of metamorphosis; "The Contrary Poet," on the character of Tristan Corbière; and "A Girl in a Library."

Jarrell published his *Selected Poems* in 1955, but only two of the poems in the book were new. It was not until 1960 that he issued a completely new book, *The Woman at the Washington Zoo*, and his readers could now see whether he was responding to the spirited technical controversies of the middle 1950's. The answer was that he had not responded at all; if anything, the new book was formally tighter than his last one. Jarrell's style had crystallized in the 1940's and had proved to be an adequate instrument for dealing with his experiences in war and peace, and he obviously felt no need to change.

The subject matter here is personal and psychological, as in *The Seven-League Crutches*. There are poems about the dull routine of ordinary urban lives and about the dreams men entertain to escape tedium. There are poems about aging, about looking backward to the always glowing past, and about the loneliness of the traveler. A number of the poems are translations from Rilke (of these, "Washing the Corpse," "Evening," and "Requiem for the Death of a Boy" are especially good), and one is a song from Goethe's *Faust*, which Jarrell intends to translate in its entirety. He should certainly be encouraged to undertake this task, for all existing translations are so incredibly bad that one doubts the value of the original.

The title poem is an ambitious attempt to enter the life of a clerk in one of the government bureaus in Washington. It is a dramatic monologue spoken by the woman as she visits the Washington Zoo and imagines herself as caged like the animals. The poem moves along convincingly—for who has not felt trapped by his job? —until the poor clerk looks up in the sky and sees a vulture, which she addresses as follows:

> Vulture,
> When you come for the white rat that the foxes left,
> Take off the red helmet of your head, the black
> Wings that have shadowed me, and step to me as man:
> The wild brother at whose feet the white wolves fawn,
> To whose hand of power the great lioness
> Stalks purring. . . .
> You know what I was,
> You see what I am: change me, change me!

Now, psychologically this is false. No woman, no matter

how caged and worthless an animal she might feel herself to be, would call upon a vulture to change or release her. The passage is clever enough, to be sure; one senses Jarrell's smile through the phallicism of the "red helmet of your head" as the vulture becomes a man. But neither the vulture's nor the clerk's metamorphosis is credible. The passage represents a failure of imagination on Jarrell's part.

No discussion of Randall Jarrell would be complete without a word about his prose. He is a literary critic of extraordinary wit and brilliance, especially notable in his demolitions of literary pretense and deflations of overblown reputations. But he is also capable of great enthusiasm; nothing excites him more than to discover merit in new poetry or to rescue masters like Whitman and Frost from neglect or defamation. His first collection of essays, *Poetry and the Age*, appeared in 1953. It consists, in part, of theoretical essays in which he attacks the public for insisting on banal comprehensibility in poetry and laughs at literary critics who build an autonomous, airy kingdom for themselves in which they can operate at a superior distance and height from the mud and agony in which creative work takes place. The other essays are in the nature of practical criticism, analyses and evaluations of the work of John Crowe Ransom, Wallace Stevens, William Carlos Williams, Robert Lowell, and Marianne Moore, among others. It is here that Jarrell offers his reasons for liking Robert

Frost, making clear how profound and complex a poem like "Design" is (but failing to see the staged symbolism of "Directive"). And it is here that he says kind words about Walt Whitman's inclusiveness of vision even as he scoffs at some of his lines:

> For instance: what other man in all the history of this planet would have said, "I am a habitan of Vienna"? (One has an immediate vision of him as a sort of French-Canadian halfbreed to whom the Viennese are offering, with trepidation, through the bars of a zoological garden, little mounds of whipped cream.)

Jarrell's next prose work was a novel, *Pictures from an Institution*; it appeared in 1954. It belongs to a popular genre, the academic novel, to which *The Groves of Academe*, by Mary McCarthy, and *Lucky Jim*, by Kingsley Amis, also belong. It is a satiric study of a progressive women's college during a year when a famous and brilliantly venomous woman novelist appears on campus to teach a course in creative writing. She is shown reacting to the vanities, hypocrisies, and absurdities of college life. Here is how Jarrell presents her as she listens to the boring, garrulous President:

> Normally she would have let a sentence or two fall on him, looked out over his squashed shape, and passed on; but now she was Collecting for the Book. She nodded; nodded; nodded again and again; nodded

until she could hardly remember whether she was agreeing or falling asleep. Now and then she would say *Yes* or *Yes?*; once when the President said something unusually absurd, she gave him a startled, grateful smile—one could see her lips move as she memorized it.

And here is how he contrasts Gertrude, the novelist, with an awkward, honest do-gooder on the staff:

After a few minutes with Gertrude you wanted to be good all day every day; after you had been with Flo you didn't know what to do—honesty and sincerity began to seem to you a dreadful thing, and you even said to yourself, like a Greek philosopher having a nervous breakdown: "Is it right to be good?"

The book is deficient in plot, and the characterization is of the sort that deduction or surmise suggests. But the style crackles and glitters with witty perceptions. It makes for enjoyable reading.

Jarrell's third volume of prose, *A Sad Heart at the Supermarket*, was published in 1962 and is the least engaging of his books. It contains a few literary essays on such writers as Rudyard Kipling and André Malraux, both of whom Jarrell admires, and an instructive autobiographical fragment in which he reveals how he wrote the poem "The Woman at the Washington Zoo." But most of the essays in the book are on such matters as anti-intellectualism in American life, Instant Literature, and the horrors of education in schools where reading matter is adjusted to the age level of pupils. These essays find Jarrell engaged in the curious activity of beating a dead horse.

The poetry and prose of Randall Jarrell make clear that he is a man of social interests. He has the eye and passions of the moralist. He writes most movingly when private and public predicaments coincide, as they did in World War II. When, in the 1950's, he turned to psychological, dream-haunted poetry, he lost the power and intensity that come from involvement in congenial subject matter. Prose then became his medium, and he produced brilliant evaluations of American literature and society. His technique as a poet developed early, in the 1940's; it was so supple that he saw little reason to change it in later years. It enabled him to write some excellent poems.

Karl Shapiro is another "social poet" who found impetus and subject matter in the public crises of the 1940's, when his private predicament as a soldier in the war against Germany and Japan merged with the predicament of American society as a whole, fighting for its survival. But, although a slow, subdued anger is the permanent emotional climate of an army, Shapiro's tone is rarely angry, even in the poems in which he points out the shortcomings of society—the racial, religious, and economic injustices that he sees about him. And, as a relatively "new" American of Jewish ancestry, he sees these very clearly. In one poem he speaks

53

of a university where "To hurt the Negro and avoid the Jew/ Is the curriculum"; in another he describes the inequalities of the graveyard, where the rich lie under ornate tombs and the poor under "machined crosses." He is bitter and ironic, but possesses enough spiritual equilibrium to be "at rest in the blast," as Marianne Moore would say. He achieves the sort of cosmic consciousness that makes possible an objectification and dramatization of inner tensions and polarities. All of his best work was done during the years 1940–1948.

Shapiro published his first book of poems in Baltimore, in 1935. It is entitled, simply, *Poems* and contains exercises in such forms as the sonnet, rondeau, triolet, and villanelle, phrased in an archaic diction heavily in debt to nineteenth-century Romantic poetry. The themes are, for the most part, traditional—love and the seasonal changes of nature—but there is an occasional reference to war and revolution in Vienna, Cuba, and China, showing that Shapiro had been "listening to the Communists." There is talk of struggle, pickets, marching; the beauty of the world "is to come," is to be built. And in the best poem in the volume, "There Are Birds," a war poem, Shapiro reveals his awareness of the coexistence of opposites in the world; he describes buzzards hanging over a battlefield and remarks, "There are also/ ever-singing/ larks not hawks."

But his first really strong work appeared in a collection of poems published by New Directions in 1941,

Five Young American Poets, Second Series. At the time of this publication Shapiro had already been inducted into the United States Army and was stationed at Camp Lee, Virginia, where he made this pronouncement: "Today American poetry suffers from the dictatorship of criticism, that branch of literature which is more devoted to dialectics than to the joyful activity of experience. Our poetry has the task of destroying the government of critics and of making a wholesale return to the anarchy of experience." This statement is the first shot in a twenty-year private war against critics, old and new, but it bears little relationship to what Shapiro actually does in his poems. Of all contemporary poets, he is the least interested in projecting "the anarchy of experience." His poems always have a point of view, often so strongly stated that it amounts to an "ideology."

For example, in "The Dome of Sunday" he expresses an almost Eliotic dislike of the modern city with its "Row-houses and row-lives." In the poem "Alexandria" his social criticism is explicitly anti-Southern and pro-Negro:

> Then let the Negroes creep out of their scars
> And enter Alexandria
> To burn the clapboard and the straw
> And cast a vote for whiteness and for trees.

In such poems as "Elegy Written on a Frontporch" and

"Midnight Show" he comments on what he regards as the horrors and obscenities of contemporary social life, and in others, like "Drug Store" and "Buick," he tries to "fix" features of the social scene in the fashion of a reporter or sociologist.

Social criticism can also be found in Shapiro's next volume, *Person, Place, and Thing*, which was issued in 1942. In a poem entitled "Property" he speaks of a familiar urban process, the devolvement of real estate from the rich to the poor as neighborhoods decay:

> Now nowhere are those tenants to be found
> Who bestowed on later citizens their oldest sections,
> But north of the city in their English valleys
> Their sons and daughters
> Continue the management of a large inheritance
> Of joy and fashion.

A note of envy seems to be present in this poem; one can almost see the stereotype of the poor boy pressing his nose against a mansion window. In another poem, "Construction," Shapiro rejects the heartless city environment of steel and concrete. In a poem entitled "& Co." he describes a man who dies spiritually in his job. In "Emporium" he shows distaste for an important feature of the business scene, the department store; in "The Snob" he attacks a "Greek-letter boy" who despises Negroes and Methodists; and in "Hollywood" he is critical of an industry that markets beauty "like a basic food."

In his next book, *V-Letter and Other Poems* (1944), Shapiro's social context expands to include the whole United States Army in the South Pacific, where the "Puritan" with his "fear/ Of beauty" moves him to mockery and where the "intellectual" appears ridiculous. Shapiro says he would rather be a milkman or a barber than an intellectual, making the curious assumption that they are mutually exclusive. (One of Shapiro's weaknesses as a poet is his predilection for categorizing people.) Among the better war poems is "The Gun," in which the weapon is seen as "the means of the practical humor of death/ Which is savage to punish the dead for the sake of my sin!" Another is "Troop Train," in which the death-haunted present of the soldier is compared with a fabulous future: "Nightfall of nations brilliant after war." One of the least successful of the war poems is "Elegy for a Dead Soldier," in which the poet's ambivalent attitude toward the man he is presumably mourning is embarrassingly evident in lines like these:

> Of all men poverty pursued him least;
> He was ashamed of all the down and out,
> And saw the unemployed as a vague mass
> Incapable of hunger or revolt.
> He hated other races, south or east,

And shoved them to the margin of his mind.
He could recall the justice of the Colt,
Take interest in a gang-war like a game.
His ancestry was somewhere far behind
And left him only his peculiar name.
. Doors opened, and he recognized no class.

This astonishing list of the dead man's prejudices ends with an epitaph:

Underneath this wooden cross there lies
A Christian killed in battle. You who read,
Remember that this stranger died in pain;
And passing here, if you can lift your eyes
Upon a peace kept by a human creed,
Know that one soldier has not died in vain.

One tends to doubt the sincerity of these lines—and yet mockery is clearly out of place in the poem. The poet is either unsure of his attitude or unwilling to be frank.

The social theme connects with the religious theme in these poems, for, as the poet remarks in his preface, "It is not the commonplace of suffering or the platitudinous comparison with the peace, or the focus on the future that should occupy us; but the spiritual progress or retrogression of the man in war, the increase or decrease in his knowledge of beauty, government and religion." Actually, some of the poems *are* built around a contrast between the past and the present or between the present and the future; such a contrast makes for a strong poetic structure. For example, in "Sunday: New Guinea" the poet describes soldiers going to church on a Sunday morning and then flashes back to intimate details of Sundays at home, where love's "presence" is "snowy, beautiful, and kind." As for "spiritual progress," it is difficult to assess movements of the spirit; but, if acceptance of death represents spiritual progress, one can point to the mail-call rumination in a poem entitled "Aside," in the course of which Shapiro says: "When and where we arrive/ Is no matter, but *how* is the question we urgently need,/ How to love and to hate, how to die, how to write and to read." And there is the title poem, "V-Letter," one of the best in the book, in which the poet makes this resounding declaration of love:

> I love you first because your years
> Lead to my matter-of-fact and simple death
> Or to our open marriage,
> And I pray nothing for my safety back,
> Not even luck, because our love is whole
> Whether I live or fail.

In many poems the religious theme is given a social emphasis through the poet's preoccupation with his identity as a Jew. Like most Americans under the pressure of influences tending toward "democratic" conformity, Shapiro responds either with a proud assertion of separateness and individuality or with a yearning for submergence, a desire to shed the difficult burden of difference. In the poem "Moses" he is proud of his heritage; addressing Moses, he says, "Converse with God made you a thinker,/ Taught us all early justice, made us a race." And in "The Synagogue" he declares, "Our name is yet the identity of God." But in the poem entitled "Jew" he speaks of the terror and bondage of history and sees the Jewish identity in this way:

> But the name is a language itself that is whispered and hissed
> Through the house of ages, and ever a language the same,
> And ever and ever a blow on our heart like a fist.

In an effort to transcend this history and to assume a comradely inclusiveness, Shapiro writes a number of poems from the Christian point of view, almost as though he were a convert. As he says in the preface, "I try to write freely, one day as a Christian, the next as a Jew, the next as a soldier who sees the slapstick of modern war." In "Christmas Eve: Australia" one finds lines like these:

> I smoke and read my Bible and chew gum,
> Thinking of Christ and Christmas of last year,
> And what those quizzical soldiers standing near

Ask of the war and Christmases to come,
And sick of causes and the tremendous blame
Curse lightly and pronounce your serious name.

In 1945 the poet published a little book entitled
Essay on Rime in which he maintains that poetry "Is in
decline" and attempts to find reasons for the decline in
"confusions" in prosody, language, and belief. He argues
for a revitalization of poetry through accessions from
the storehouses of prose, opposes the poetry of ideas,
and lines up with the common man in his suspicion of
modern poetry, aiming to "solidify/ The layman's confidence in a plainer art." Written for the author's own
amusement while he was on a tour of duty in New
Guinea, the book is, nevertheless, full of affectations,
such as the archaic title, which refers not to rhyme, as
one would suppose, but to poetry in general. The mar-
gins of the text are spotted with topic titles, as though
the author were afraid that the reader would be unable
to follow the close reasoning of the argument without
their aid. Actually, the book is banal and very badly
argued. The quality of the verse can be judged by these
lines on the meter of the poem:

The metric of this book is made upon
The classic English decasyllable
Adapted to the cadence of prose speech;
Ten units to the verse by count of eye
Is the ground rhythm, over which is set
The rougher flux and reflux of conversation.

In his next book, *Trial of a Poet* (1947), Shapiro returns to his exploration of the social context of religious experience. Here, in "The Convert," he describes sympathetically a man's conversion to Catholicism despite "The groan of positive science, hiss of friends"; the convert knows how heavy "the hand that hates" is and "How light and secret is the sign of love." But a very different view of conversion is presented in "Recapitulations," a seemingly autobiographical poem which traces the poet's development and contains these bitter lines:

> Two priests advised me on my rise to grace,
> The one among the sacred bric-a-brac
> Questioning my devotion to my face,
> The other frankly dubious of my race.

Another aspect of the social scene that interests Shapiro in this, his first postwar, volume is the adjustment of the soldier to civilian life, as in the poem "Demobilization," where, speaking for all returned soldiers, he says:

> Saviors and spies, we seek the road we lost
> When kidnapped from indifference. As before,
> Back where I started from, I stare, touch wood.

And, now that the war is over, he takes a generous view

of conscientious objectors; they are equal in heroism with the men who died in combat:

> Well might the soldier kissing the hot beach
> Erupting in his face damn all your kind.
> Yet you who save neither yourselves nor us
> Are equally with those who shed the blood
> The heroes of our cause. Your conscience is
> What we come back to in the armistice.

In other poems he is less generous. In "Boy-Man," for example, he describes a male type that he dislikes, and in "The Southerner" he pictures a man who knows how to conform and to compel and who still denies "the fall/ Of Richmond and man." In some poems he touches on the social meaning of technological advance, as in "Air Liner" and "The Progress of Faust." In the latter poem the age-old Faustian lust for knowledge spends itself in the orgasm of an atomic explosion in the desert.

Clearly, all these poems of the 1940's have their social meaning. Ideologically, they seem to be liberal, and the formulations of political and social attitude, the abstractions of an intellect at work in categories, owe a great deal to W. H. Auden, who, ironically enough, had already abandoned his liberalism by 1941. Shapiro owes a great deal to Auden in matters of technique also, in his handling of stanza and line, for, like Auden, he works in traditional measures, knowing that a relatively prosaic content requires meter. Within traditional limits he enjoys experiments, particularly in anapaestic measure. This return to formalism was characteristic of American poetry during the late 1940's and early 1950's; as Shapiro remarks in *English Prosody and Modern Poetry* (1947), "Many of our best poets have led a return to verse structures which twenty years ago were held to be dead and gone." For the most part, Shapiro does well with these structures, but now and then he produces incredible verses like this stanza from "Recapitulations":

> Doctors and cousins paid their call,
> The rabbi and my father helped.
> A crucifix burned on the wall
> Of the bright room where I was whelped.

Reading these lines, one despairs of meter, rhyme, and poetry in general. One feels like joining Marianne Moore when she confesses that she, too, dislikes poetry.

In 1953, as though to signal the end of an epoch, Shapiro published his *Poems, 1940–1953*. Only five of the poems in the collection were new, and of these the best poem, "Israel," had been written in 1948 to celebrate the founding of the state of Israel and was read at a political meeting in Baltimore in the same year. This "occasional" poem, inspired by a political development in the Near East, marks a turning point in Shapiro's attitude toward his Jewish heritage. Whatever ambivalence may have been present in earlier years is now gone; he is clearly proud of his people and the new state of Israel. He says, "When I see the name of Israel high in print/ The fences crumble in my flesh." And he adds, "I say my name/ Aloud for the first time unconsciously." This is a remarkable change when one considers that, as a beginning writer, Shapiro once wrote to a fellow poet to ask him "what obstacles one had to overcome to publish poems under a Jewish name." The poem ends on a very positive note:

> Speak of the tillage of a million heads
> No more. Speak of the evil myths no more
> Of one who harried Jesus on his way
> Saying, *Go faster*. Speak no more
> Of the yellow badge, *secta nefaria*.
> Speak the name only of the living land.

The most ambitious poem in the book is a retelling of the story of Adam and Eve in rhymed iambic pentameter. The poem belongs to the new trend in the immediate postwar years toward psychological explorations with a mythological emphasis and relies for its imagery on the Bible, the *Zohar*, and the writings of Wilhelm Reich. Its thesis, according to Shapiro himself, is that "man is for the world, not for the afterworld," but this thesis is so muted—and, indeed, it is contradicted by Eve, who prays to God, "Guide us to Paradise," in the hour of the pair's expulsion from Eden—that it seems like an afterthought. And the verse is easy, facile, and without the precise imagery that makes for visual immediacy.

In 1958, Shapiro published another book, *Poems of a Jew*, which contains twenty-seven poems that had appeared in earlier collections and six new poems, all of them on the familiar social-religious theme that is dominant in the poet's work. The importance of the collection lies in the poet's proud assertion of his identity as a Jew. The nature of this identity is clear enough from the poems themselves, with their vivid social, historical, and religious imagery, but the poet further clarifies it in the introduction to the book: "As everyone knows, a Jew who becomes an atheist remains a Jew. A Jew who becomes a Catholic remains a Jew. Being a Jew is the consciousness of being a Jew, and the Jewish identity, with or without religion, with or without history, is the significant fact." This identity involves an "intimacy" with God, according to Shapiro, but not necessarily with Judaism; it represents worldliness; and it can be equated with "the primitive ego of the human race."

A look through his books reveals that Shapiro published only eleven new poems between 1948 and 1958, either because of the uncongeniality of the period or because of the pressure of his teaching duties and editorial chores. (He was editor of *Poetry* for five years.) He did manage to publish a book of prose, however; this was *Beyond Criticism* (1953), in which he fulminates against all literary dogmas because they are "ruinous to poetry" and attacks "slavery to doctrines of culture under the guise of history and myth" because they lead to the destruction of personality in art. In practice, of course, his own poems frequently invoke social, literary, and historical contexts.

In 1960, Shapiro published a collection of critical essays, *In Defense of Ignorance*, which he says is his last: "The present essays are intended to be the last criticism I shall ever write." In this book Shapiro takes up his lifelong war against critics, intellectuals, and all members of what he calls the "Modernist School," which includes William Butler Yeats, Ezra Pound, and T. S. Eliot. Dismissing all poetry that betrays the impress of ideas or the control of a mind, he declares that "poetry has lost its significance, its relevance, and even its meaning in our time. To begin again it must repair to the wilderness, outside society, outside the city gates, a million miles from books and their keepers." It is clear that he favors the cosmic individualism of such writers as Walt Whitman and Henry Miller and the spontaneity and immediacy of William Carlos Williams. The secret of form, according to Shapiro, is "the eradication of the line between poetry and prose, between life and art."

These pronouncements suggest the poet's awareness of the new spontaneous poetry of the late 1950's and betray his uneasiness over his own carefully measured poetry of the 1940's. A study of the poems in *The Bourgeois Poet* (1964) shows that Shapiro is now writing a very prosaic free verse but that his subject matter is unchanged: he still writes social commentaries, as the very title of his book indicates. His poems have, in the past, been saved from prose by an underpinning of meter; now he has the problem of creating a strong substitute rhythm that can organize his essentially prosaic subject matter.

There is no doubt that Shapiro's best work belongs to the years 1940–1948, when he wrote "Necropolis," "Buick," "University," "Waitress," "Auto Wreck," "Troop Train," "The Gun," "Jew," "The Leg," "V-Letter," "The Conscientious Objector," "The Convert," and "Israel." But these poems are in traditional measures, on which the poet has now turned his back.

Elizabeth Bishop is not a poet who finds inspiration in
public events, political issues, or socioeconomic ideology; reading her, one is unaware of Hitler and World
War II, just as one is unaware of Napoleon and his wars
when reading the works of Jane Austen. Unlike many
of her Auden-influenced contemporaries, she distrusts
history, with its melodramatic blacks and whites, and
prefers geography, with its subtle gradations of color.
As she says in "The Map," the opening poem in *North
and South*, "Topography displays no favorites; North's
as near as West./ More delicate than the historians' are

69

the map makers' colors." And, like a geographer, she delights in the landscapes, animals, customs, climates, and changing lights of the world, which are very real to her: she is no solipsist. Her sense of the existence of objects relates her to William Carlos Williams and, especially, to Marianne Moore, who has a similar passion for precise rendering of the scenes and inhabitants of the world. Restless as an explorer or a tourist, Miss Bishop moves along many roads in search of objects and insights, and such various places as Florida, New England, Paris, New York, Cape Breton, Washington, and Santos become subjects for her poems.

As a peripatetic poet and geographer, Miss Bishop avoids that concentration on the self which often leads to emotion that "too far exceeds its cause," like that which a map maker perhaps feels as he runs the names of cities across neighboring mountains. Perhaps it is an extraordinary vulnerability that makes her look outward rather than inward. At any rate, she registers those increments of awareness that experience of many latitudes brings. Her verse does not lack feeling—it is merely directed to the objects that elicit feeling. These objects point to the ambiguities, beauty, and suffering of a world subject to time and death. Time is said to be like the sea in a poem entitled "The Unbeliever": it "wants to destroy us all." Like Joseph Conrad, Miss Bishop counsels courageous immersion. As for the prizes of the world—she has the morality and magnanimity of a patrician who, having caught a fish, forgoes his advantage and lets it go.

The poet's characteristics are fully evident in her first book, *North and South*, which appeared in 1946 and contained poems written mostly before 1942. It reveals her wonder and excitement as she looks at the world and describes what she sees. Some of this excitement derives from her discovery that language can perform miracles of exactness in description. One can actually see the shadow of a man in moonlight with the aid of these lines:

> The whole shadow of Man is only as big as his hat.
> It lies at his feet like a circle for a doll to stand on,
> and he makes an inverted pin, the point magnetized to
>   the moon.

Here are some sharp observations of a sprinkler at work in New York City:

> Along the street below
> the water-wagon comes
>
> throwing its hissing, snowy fan across
> peelings and newspapers. The water dries
>   light-dry, dark-wet, the pattern
>   of the cool watermelon.

And how astonishingly audible is the crowing of cocks
in this passage:

> At four o'clock
> in the gun-metal blue dark
> we hear the first crow of the first cock
>
> just below
> the gun-metal blue window
> and immediately there is an echo
>
> off in the distance,
> then one from the back-yard fence,
> then one, with horrible insistence,
>
> grates like a wet match
> from the broccoli patch,
> flares, and all over town begins to catch.

Much of the effectiveness of these descriptions derives, of course, from the figures of speech, from the
correspondences that the poet discovers between the
objects she is describing and other objects, not present,
that her imagination entertains. For example, who be-
sides Miss Bishop has ever seen a relationship between
the grating sound of a wet match and the croak of a
cock at dawn? One often finds such a delighted yoking
together of disparate elements. In the following lines
the poet compares two peninsulas drawn on a map to
the fingers of women examining cloth:

These peninsulas take the water between thumb and
    finger
like women feeling for the smoothness of yard-goods.

And in this passage she sees the wake of a barge as an
oak leaf:

Each barge on the river easily tows
    a mighty wake,
a giant oak-leaf of gray lights
    on duller gray . . .

This power of imaginative description is put at the
service of Miss Bishop's insights into the commonest of
experiences, among them mortality. Significantly, love
is, for her, a burning boy on the deck of a burning ship
trying to recite "The boy stood on the burning deck."
The boy is perhaps anyone yearning for the ideal that
love and art represent even as he and the world around
him suffer the processes of time, the flames that are the
joy and doom of all living things. In love with human
love, Miss Bishop is nevertheless aware of inconstancy
and inconsistency and sometimes listens ironically to
what men say about love. In "Chemin de Fer," for example, she describes a hunter-hermit who shoots off his
shotgun even as he screams, "Love should be put into
action!" The poet remarks, wryly, "Across the pond an
echo/ tried and tried to confirm it."

And nature itself is ambiguous in Miss Bishop's conception. In some of the poems the sea is hostile, destructive; it is said to resemble a case of knives. But the sun in "Anaphora" is benign; it sets behind a beggar in the park as "the fiery event/ of every day in endless/ endless assent." The ambiguity is especially evident in the poem "Roosters," in which the sun makes his appearance after a battle of cocks: "The sun climbs in,/ following 'to see the end,'/ faithful as enemy, or friend."

Miss Bishop loves the world for whatever virtue and beauty she can find in it, content with much less than all. In support of this assertion one can cite the witty poem "The Gentlemen of Shalott," in which the symmetry of a man's body is said to imply a mirror at his spine: a man is really only half of himself. And the protagonist of the poem concludes that "Half is enough."

Most of the poems in *North and South* are strikingly imagined and ordered, but, now and then, as in the case of the poem "Florida," the poet's exuberance provides a scattering of images whose relevance to the total structure is open to question. It is as though Miss Bishop stopped along the road home to examine every buttercup and asphodel she saw. The images are dazzling; they call attention to themselves like ambitious actors in minor roles; but they contribute very little to the total effect. Some of the descriptive poems are saved from disintegration by a metaphor, an apt unifying image, in the concluding lines.

The poems fall into three categories of rhythmic organization. Some of them are in traditional metrical patterns; "Chemin de Fer," for example, is in iambic-trimeter quatrains rhyming abcb:

> Alone on the railroad track
> I walked with pounding heart.
> The ties were too close together
> or maybe too far apart.

Much more characteristic of Miss Bishop's work are the free-verse poems, which move in easy rhythms. Here are the opening lines of "The Fish," an extraordinary achievement in rendering the heroism of simple survival—that of a fish with "five old pieces of fish-line" stuck in its lip:

> I caught a tremendous fish
> and held him beside the boat
> half out of water, with my hook
> fast in a corner of his mouth.
> He didn't fight.
> He hadn't fought at all.
> He hung a grunting weight . . .

The "I" character admires this old battler so much that, in the end, she lets it go. The lines are free verse, ·no doubt, but it should be noted that, with the exception of the fifth line, there are clusters of three stresses in each line. In other poems there are clusters of two or four or five stresses, with an irregular number of unaccented syllables between the stresses, suggesting that Miss Bishop likes accentual verse, perhaps because of the "sprung" effect it permits her to achieve.

Miss Bishop published her second book, *Poems*, in 1955. The work contained all of the poems in *North and South* and a new group entitled "A Cold Spring," which was written in the years 1942–1955. The new poems, like the old, are rich in reports of the colors, shapes, and temperatures of the world; they contain vivid contrasts, sometimes held in paradoxical suspension as unities, as in the juxtaposition of winter and spring in "A Cold Spring," a poem in which cold weather points to a summer lit by fireflies. And there is a considerable variety of scene; Miss Bishop is still a tourist, examining the farmyards and shores of New England, a port in Brazil, and the Capitol in Washington, among other places. As usual, she provides illumination by way of description; she searches out realities and comes upon truths. The emblem is always there, but not to the neglect of the real scene, the toad in the imaginary garden. Light radiates through the scene, and the ultimate effect is a kind of inwardness, after all, like that of Anne Bradstreet contemplating a New England wilderness. She sometimes begins her descriptive details casually, hopefully, not really knowing where they might lead, and then, suddenly, the fish leaps in the sun, the miracle of poetic insight is achieved.

Again, as in *North and South*, it is the beauty, pain, wealth, poverty, and sorrow of a world caught in the processes of time that stir Miss Bishop; she is indifferent to politics. When she writes about Washington, D.C., it is not to make a comment on the political scene or to describe congressmen in debate, but, rather, to suggest the power of the sun and the trees. In one of the best poems in the book, "View of the Capitol from the Library of Congress," she describes an Air Force band playing loudly but ineffectually over a long distance: "The giant trees stand in between." The trees catch "the music in their leaves." The poem ends as follows:

> Great shades, edge over,
> give the music room.
> The gathered brasses want to go
> *boom—boom.*

How wittily and yet how seriously that "boom" echoes! Perhaps it implies a comment on government, war, and military force, after all!

As a determined traveler on the roads of the world, Miss Bishop keeps noting ironies, in Washington as in Santos, Brazil. Speaking of the tourist mentality in "Arrival at Santos," she notes the "immodest demands for a different world,/ and a better life, and complete comprehension/ of both at last, and immediately." She intends humor here, but there is no doubt that she, too, makes demands on the world. But she knows its limits, accepts them, finally, and, finding the port of Santos unattractive, drives on "to the interior."

The central poem of the new group is "At the Fishhouses," an elaborate description of the rocks, lights, fish tubs, and waters of a New England fishing town, featuring an old man, who is a friend of the speaker's grandfather, and also a seal that is "interested in music." The poem begins in seemingly undirected fashion and pauses to examine whatever Miss Bishop's eye lights upon, but then it moves more slowly and mounts in emotional power as the waters of the bay come into view. It ends with this passage on the sea:

> It is like what we imagine knowledge to be:
> dark, salt, clear, moving, utterly free,
> drawn from the cold hard mouth
> of the world, derived from the rocky breasts
> forever, flowing and drawn, and since
> our knowledge is historical, flowing, and flown.

This ending is not quite inevitable; it is not really prepared for; but it tells brilliantly what Miss Bishop thinks of human knowledge, which is always undermined by time, by change. It is obvious that change is the most disturbing principle of reality for her. The poem is a good one; it invokes a scene and a way of life and invests them with meaning.

Another poem, "Cape Breton," provides a similar dazzle of descriptive details and suffers from a similar lack of inevitability. The poem moves without tension through a landscape across which a bus rolls, crowded with people. It ends with this fine but not at all inclusive image: "an ancient chill is rippling the dark brooks." This ending is in marked contrast to the effective last lines of a poem entitled "Bight" which describes a seashore scene: "All the untidy activity continues,/ awful but cheerful." It is an amused, not unkindly, and fairly accurate characterization of the world.

Clearly, then, Elizabeth Bishop is a poet who, early in her career, chose to avoid politics and public issues without, at the same time, abandoning the objective realities that constitute the otherness of the world. She believes in that world, especially when it shocks or baffles her, and she renders it with precision and clarity. By 1955 the interchange between self and scene deepens in her poems, and her love of geography takes her, as tourist and everyman, to many places on many roads.

[6] *JEAN GARRIGUE*

Even as an undergraduate at the University of Chicago, in the middle 1930's, when she participated in the heady controversies of the Poetry Club, which then included such poets as Paul Goodman, Ruth Herschberger, and Edouard Roditi, Jean Garrigue was a magician of words, profoundly in love with her medium. Her silken lines had a controlled metrical music and a sumptuous imagery that made the work of most of her contemporaries seem grimy in comparison. But her commitment to her craft did not signify an indifference to the world and its social and economic problems. Like some other poets of her generation, she responded strongly to the great ills of the depression decade and the war years; but she transmuted them, gave them a timeless cast, and made them part of the moral environment of individuals caught in private dilemmas. In her first collection of poems, "Thirty-Six Poems and a Few Songs," which appeared in *Five Young American Poets*, Third Series, in 1944, the emphasis is on the transports and agonies of the individual beset by warring opposites, inner and outer. He is pictured as surrounded by a dangerous, sick world that is symbolized by woods that "lock us up/ In the secret crimes of our intent." It is clear that both the will or "intent" and the outer world are responsible for what happens. That is why the forest takes on the moral character of Dante's "Inferno" in "The Circle," a poem that is full of the imagery of decay and projects an eternity of terror in a dark wood "swollen with mushrooms." It is, perhaps, a lack of faith or trust in others that makes the world dangerous; in "The Park," at any rate, people are said to be strangers to one another and doomed:

> Like strangers forced by hate, we greet
> Who find no saving faith before the brink
> And have plunged down into its boiling dark.

The phrase "boiling dark" suggests the gloom of W. B. Yeats in "The Second Coming"; like him, Miss Garrigue sees that the "ceremony of innocence" has been drowned. She also sees that people are afraid of the truth and keep it at a distance from themselves until night brings "the dreaded smile of honesty." But there are positive moments in experience also, sudden glimpses of ideal form, beauty, that suggest an eternity beyond sorrow, as in the figure of a woman who walks like a dancer in the moving poem entitled "The Stranger."

A poem is a means of preserving these glimpses of beauty as well as other elements of experience. As Miss Garrigue says, "Suppose his [the poet's] first motivation is to conserve, preserve—the leaf that is about to fall—to arrest a time at its perfection, to isolate, even to 'refrigerate' it, to justify the dear vanity of infatuation with sensation, pleasure, appearance, by making the object perennially accessible to, perennially violent, magnetic, bristling with the activities and ambivalences of insight."

The themes of the first collection are renewed in the second, *The Ego and the Centaur*, which was published in 1947. Here it is clear that the poet is weary of war, political ideology, and duty—the sacrifice of personal good for the general welfare. She stresses the values of a free personal life, too long denied. In the opening poem of the book, "The Soldiers, the Birds and the Monuments," she describes a park scene in which she contrasts a squad of soldiers, "springing with clipped tread," with a flock of pigeons which, disturbed by the soldiers, rise in a "drunken rush" past "slipshod citizens." It is obvious that she prefers the pigeons and the slipshod citizens to the soldiers; she remarks, "For who who sees the birds rage off/ Sees not his freedom and his choice prorogued?" Later she implies that "Our anarchistic loves" bolt with the birds.

Miss Garrigue's preference for the intense, particular reality of the private life is also evident in "Oration Against the Orator's Oration," in which she attacks all windy argument and defends the "five green senses" and the "naked, maculate and faulty" world that they report. Her remarks are so vehement that she seems to be arguing against the reason itself, as in this ironic passage:

> I see the world, it's propped by argument,
> Vast pillars set to support a windy pride,
> Pediments acanthus-bound, entablatures,
> All ways to keep the ego up and sun
> As if we couldn't bear the world
> Unpropped, unbooked, and unreasoned.

And yet she is aware of the havoc that sensation and emotion, unhampered and untroubled by "right reason," can produce. The war itself is an example. In the poem "V-J Day" she expresses relief at the end of the wholesale butchery of the war, which released base instincts and generated unbearable guilts:

Eternal beasts make guiltless none of us
This thought resents us and disheartens tears.
We know no one exactly to address.
Sensations, brutalized, are more helpless
At hoping to invoke the name of Love.

By the end of the poem she finds that she must, never-theless, rely on love, an as-if belief in love, in order that the guilt-ridden conscience may win a measure of peace.

The free, independent life that Miss Garrigue celebrates is not without its turbulences, anxieties, and complexities. To suggest its contradictions she moves into the conjectural domain of the centaur, which is the focal symbol of the book. The centaur is the "Adam of improbables," but one can infer truths about oneself by studying his "Protean selves" and "Himalayan op-posites." These opposites can be put in traditional terms as reason and passion, man and animal, the ideal and the real, love and hate.

The disturbances that these opposites set in motion make for the drama of the love poems, in one of which the "I" character cries out that desire clouds her sight "In willful ignorances throughout!" In another poem the speaker remarks, ruefully, that "Captivity is tor-ment that we want"; in still another she addresses her lover in these terms: "Abyss, who harbors my infirmi-ties,/ The angels of your eyes are all my foes." And, in a more abstract style, Miss Garrigue's lover defines arrogance by invoking its opposite, humility:

> Arrogance is the humility and mystery
> That let you permit me in time
> Find the fire that will burn me through.

The dualities of the self, in a particular range and measure, make for the uniqueness that we know as an individual. The lover values it in his loved one because, in his ecstasy, he feels that she is unrepeatable; but when rarity verges on eccentricity, as in the case of adaptations that are not useful or viable, neither the lover nor society approves. The outcast lives unhappily with his difference, his oddity, "like old continents/ Unmodified and discontinued." Miss Garrigue expresses love and pity for the rare being and sympathizes with his frustration at his incompatibility with the world in which he finds himself. She makes this clear in her poem "False Country of the Zoo," which opens with these lines:

> We are large with pity, slow and awkward,
> In the false country of the zoo.
> For the beasts our hearts turn over and sigh.
> With the gazelle we long to look eye to eye.
> Laughter at the stumbling, southern giraffes
> Urges our anger, righteous despair.

It is the ideal world that provides a contrast to the disappointments and errors of the real one. The existence of this ideal world is postulated on an as-if basis; it is a necessity of the imagination because, as the poet says in "Primer of Plato," "All endeavor to be beautiful." The Platonic sky of forms can be induced from glimpses of beauty on earth and then made to serve as a pattern for the objects and activities of ordinary reality. This is abundantly clear in "Movie Montage," a brilliantly realized poem in which a movie theater serves as the Platonic cave where the spectator, watching a Western, attempts to join the ideal and the real:

> To set the body down in images:
> That is what we strive, we struggle for,
> To render from an ideality
> The lust of senators and buffaloes

The Ego and the Centaur is a book with the affecting strangeness of the very individuality it celebrates; it deals with the world everyone knows, and yet it has the otherworldliness of experience raised several degrees above the expected and ordinary. It has a musicality, a refinement, and an elegance of phrase that are appealing and rare. It aims for a fullness of rhetoric reminiscent of the Elizabethans. Its deficiencies can be listed as a rather tricky syntax; a coy archaism of diction that results from a sense of the inadequacy of the contemporary vocabulary in any act of conjuring; and a tendency to abstraction and philosophy in situations that could be made much more vivid by rendering.

Miss Garrigue's next book, *The Monument Rose*, appeared in 1953. It contains highly personal, full-voiced, essentially romantic lyrics in which the poet's love of her medium and her self-confidence in handling it are evident. One feels a tremendous excitement in the poems, and at a singing intensity that only a fully awake sensibility could sustain. But these are not poems of innocence, in William Blake's sense; they are poems of experience, for they encompass not only the wonders of the world of the senses but also the mind's retreat from them. In a way, they represent an attempt at assessing the limits of romanticism. Miss Garrigue remembers the warring opposites of reality. She projects a contrast between what was and what is, between hope and despair, between life and death. In the love poems positive and negative emotions coexist. For example, in "For Anybody's Martyr's Song," the speaker asks resignedly: "Children hate school, soldiers discipline/ Love hates love but what's the good of that?" She describes her mistreatment by her lover in these terms:

> [Love] Indulges with contempt your sweet tooth at the
> fair,
> Gives you fearful rides on the roller coaster,
> Greets you like a sovereign when you've come

An hour, but puts the green toad in your bed
Just as soon thereafter.
Your sober love turns tomcat in the bar.

She ends the poem with the remark that love accepts
what love is as one accepts a leopard-spotted reality.

Another favorite theme of Miss Garrigue's, the
plight of the individual under pressure of a hostile or
unbearably efficient environment, finds expression in
"The Little Pony." Here the poet commiserates with a
pony forced to carry kicking and bawling children
around a track; she describes him as stumbling but still
possessing an admirable vehemence and pride. The
poem concludes in this way:

How save the pony that he not be maimed
Beyond redemption and recall,
His low broad nostril and his waiting back
A taunt to those afflicted by their lack,
To whips the gash, to power the gall,
And despot law.

The pony is, no doubt, an emblem of the trammeled
spirit suffering under the whips of "despot law." One
gathers, despite the tricky syntax, that the pony is the
"gall" to power and despot law. One senses Miss Garrigue's emotional involvement in the plight of the pony
through the subtle shift from the interrogative mode
to the declarative mode (the passage ends with a period,

not, as one would expect, with a question mark) and in the short, emphatic conclusion.

Given the world as she describes it, one is not surprised to find Miss Garrigue engaged in constructing an ideal order to which she can raise her eyes. It is a requisite of her emotional life. For example, "Invocation to Old Windylocks" is an ecstatic celebration of a mountain that represents "The energy of our unearthly hopes" and so takes on the attributes of God. These attributes are not all positive, to be sure; the poet speaks of the mountain's "steeps and falls" and "rigor" and sees in it a primal ambivalence reminiscent of Moby-Dick. Nevertheless, she admires it, holds "infatuate" to its flank, calls it "Great prow, aërial bulk," and "Arcana coelestia." At the root of her admiration is a desire to be at one with the great forces of the universe, of eternity, which encompasses all the ambivalences of reality.

The unhappiness of the man who cannot achieve union with these universal forces, who is caught in a reality with limits, is suggested in the poem "The Maimed Grasshopper Speaks Up," in which a grasshopper is represented as possessing "three simple eyes" that permit it to see only what is "Up close." It is unable to see backward or forward or upward because "The biggest eyes" cannot serve it; "the armor's broke." What it sees cannot satisfy the brain, which "asks for eyes that see all round." The poem ends on this note of prayer or aspiration:

Universalists of sight,
I to that moon am like the blind
Who may but feel, not see its light.
And thus in destitution sit.

World without end, commend me to your might
That I my simple eyes may set
On it, or death, or hate, and get some light.

There are irony and poignancy in this aspiration because, as the poet knows, "simple eyes" cannot "see all round" except by miracle.

After 1953, Miss Garrigue traveled widely in Europe, and the record of her journeys is to be found in her next book, *A Water Walk by Villa d'Este*, which came out in 1959. It is a meditative, relaxed, sometimes talkative account of the sights and sounds of Paris, Florence, Rome, and other places. It is a much less satisfactory book than, say, *The Monument Rose* because the description lacks tension and dramatic relevance; it does not relate to any profound inner need, even though the poet works mightily to freight it with significance, as in the poem entitled "For the Fountains and Fountaineers of Villa d'Este," to which she devotes eight pages of rhetoric.

In the best poems one finds the familiar tension of opposites. In "The Hunt," for example, Miss Garrigue contrasts the life of art with the life of pleasure, personifying them as beasts, one aerial, the other earthly.

She expresses her preference for the aerial beast, even though it comes "from lofts beyond the skies/ Where stay all banished mysteries." And in another poem of contrasts, "One for the Roses," Miss Garrigue combines images of red roses and of November wind and snow, observing, at the poem's end, that the red rose is the light and day of an "absolute dominion" that is beyond all weather.

The absolute, the ideal world still enlists the allegiance of the poet, though it seems increasingly a postulate, an illusion. To suggest its remoteness and yet its attractiveness, Miss Garrigue makes it the subject of a grandmother's monologue, "What My Grandmother Said When She Fed the Kingdoms of the Air." The grandmother is a believer; she thinks that the mysterious coming of birds to be fed at her window in winter (how did they know that the bread was on the window sill?) implies the oneness of the universe and the existence of a directing God:

> Because you fly from what I do not know
> And come so sudden here
> By roads exact of wind and light
> I call invisible,
> You make me think there is
> Somehow an indivisible thing to share,
> Pastures and for someone's care,
> If you and world and I could know
> In this dark snow.

Miss Garrigue's most recent book, *Country Without Maps* (1964), represents an elaboration of the themes and attitudes of *A Water Walk by Villa d'Este*. It contains one of her best poems, "Her Spring Song," in which an old woman planting rosebushes is shown thinking back on the enchantments and heartbreak of her life.

Clearly, it is Jean Garrigue's lyricism and technical brilliance that make her visions persuasive and distinctive. Although her commitment to verbal magic sometimes draws her into a forest of rhetoric from which too much contemporary reality is banned, she succeeds in conveying, in her best poems, a sense of the world's dangers and delights.

In discussing the attributes of the poet, Aristotle praised the gift of metaphor-making, the power to fuse the elements of a scattered or fragmented reality into meaningful new unities. Richard Wilbur has that gift, that power, and, in addition, the patience and perseverance of the craftsman, the carpenter, who respects his medium and submits himself to the slow task of fitting matter to design, theme to object. This combination of qualities has enabled him to write poems that are eminently well made: they are brilliant, strong in structure, and elegant. He works in traditional metrical forms and stanzas because, as he puts it, "The strength of the genie comes of his being confined in a bottle." He evidently likes the resistance that formal obstacles represent and enjoys the triumph that makes them seem easy. It is perhaps this commitment to the forms, the nets, of tradition that enables him to sing. In this he is unlike many of his contemporaries, who merely talk.

He published his first book, *The Beautiful Changes,* in 1947. It contains forty-two poems written during the eventful years 1943–1947, but only six of them are on subjects directly related to the war, and these are among the less stirring poems in the volume. It must be said that public issues have not been particularly fruitful sources of subject matter for Mr. Wilbur, although he returns to them again and again, apparently feeling duty-bound to show his readers that he, too, worries about the atom bomb and the injustices of the McCarran Act. At any rate, a few of the war poems deserve to be noted. In "Mine Country," Wilbur sympathizes with European children who cannot cross pastures and woods without fear of exploding hidden mines, left there by soldiers to kill their enemies, and comments sorrowfully on the difficulty of "disinheriting" these children of a gruesome past and teaching them to trust the things of the world again. The poem entitled "Potato" is a tribute to the common potato, which kept the French people alive during the war years: it has "second-rate flowers" that are "beautiful only to hunger." And in "Place Pigalle," Wilbur presents a soldier talking to a girl whom he has picked up in Paris; through him the poet expresses the duality of man, his killing and his creating:

> "Girl, if I love thee not, then let me die;
> Do I not scorn to change my state with kings?
> Your muchtouched flesh, incalculable, which wrings
> Me so, now shall I gently seize in my
> Desperate soldier's hands which kill all things."

For the most part, the book is a joyous celebration of all that is wild and free and full of life. Wilbur praises the moral-free singing of the grasshopper, the nearly gravity-free leap of a sailboat in a race, the wild luxuriance of a garden which triumphs over all walls. He takes pleasure in the beauty of objects, for "the beautiful changes/ In such kind ways," and delights in all particularities, rarities, and oddities. He regrets the passing of the dodo:

> Dive, dodo, on the earth you left forlorn,
> Sit vastly on the branches of our trees,
> And chant us grandly all improbabilities.

He enjoys the play of the imagination, the ability to see summer where winter rules, a dazzle of light where there is gloom, for such play suggests a "prime/ In the heart." Understandably, he rejects abstraction, the circles of geometry, liking them only when they return to nature and borrow flesh and content from it. He makes his point in a sonnet entitled "O":

> The idle dayseye, the laborious wheel,
> The osprey's tours, the pointblank matin sun
> Sanctified first the circle; thence for fun
> Doctors deduced a shape, which some called real
> (So all games spoil), a shape of spare appeal,
> Cryptic and clean, and endlessly spinning unspun.
> Now I go backward, filling by one and one
> Circles with hickory spokes and rich soft shields
> Of petalled dayseyes, with herehastening steel
> Volleys of daylight, writhing white looks of sun;
> And I toss circles skyward to be undone
> By actual wings, for wanting this repeal
> I should go whirling a thin Euclidean reel,
> No hawk or hickory to true my run.

This poem is not as smoothly shaped as some of the others in the book—for example, "Tywater" or "Cigales." It loses some of its force through the change of direction that begins in the twelfth line with the phrase "for wanting this repeal." This reversal offers another image of an abstract circle and dams the flow of positive emotion that was directed to circles with content. But the poem admirably suggests Wilbur's love of the things of this world, their textures and colors, and his distrust of fleshless abstraction.

This love of concrete reality, of particulars, is

evident also in *Ceremony* (1950), a deftly written, fluent book full of the poet's experience of objects under varying conditions of light and weather. In "La Rose des Vents," for example, a fanciful Poet suggests to his Lady that they "dwell/ On the rose of the winds," and the practical, world-loving Lady replies:

> Forsake those roses
> Of the mind
> And tend the true,
> The mortal flower.

In "Castles and Distances," Wilbur praises a Duke who gives up his pursuit of the mysteries of a receding horizon for the sake of local mastery in a world of "advocates and enemies." But the best expression of Wilbur's love of actuality, with all its contrasts, is to be found in " 'A World Without Objects Is a Sensible Emptiness' ":

> The tall camels of the spirit
> Steer for their deserts, passing the last groves loud
> With the sawmill shrill of the locust, to the whole
>   honey of the arid
> Sun. They are slow, proud,
>
> And move with a stilted stride
> To the land of sheer horizon, hunting Traherne's
> *Sensible emptiness*, there where the brain's lantern-slide
> Revels in vast returns.

O connoisseurs of thirst,
Beasts of my soul who long to learn to drink
Of pure mirage, those prosperous islands are accurst
That shimmer on the brink

Of absence; auras, lustres,
And all shinings need to be shaped and borne.
Think of those painted saints, capped by the early
masters
With bright, jauntily-worn

Aureate plates, or even
Merry-go-round rings. Turn, O turn
From the fine sleights of the sand, from the long empty
oven
Where flames in flamings burn

Back to the trees arrayed
In bursts of glare, to the halo-dialing run
Of the country creeks, and the hills' bracken tiaras made
Gold in the sunken sun,

Wisely watch for the sight
Of the supernova burgeoning over the barn,
Lampshine blurred in the steam of beasts, the spirit's
right
Oasis, light incarnate.

This beautifully structured poem moves from the thirst
of the "tall camels of the spirit" loping toward mirages
on the horizon to an image of a barn in which "lampshine" blurs "in the steam of beasts," which the poet

calls "the spirit's right/ Oasis." He values the embodiment of spirit even though the body is maculate.

But the substantiality of the body is open to question, of course, and for a man of imagination Bishop Berkeley's philosophy has a strong appeal. In some of his poems Wilbur entertains the notion that reality is merely the point at which subject and object coincide. Here, for example, is what he says in his poem "Epistemology":

I

Kick at the rock, Sam Johnson, break your bones:
But cloudy, cloudy is the stuff of stones.

II

We milk the cow of the world, and as we do
We whisper in her ear, "You are not true."

This thought teases one into conceding the possibility that the celebration of the things of this world is, in reality, a celebration of the individual imagination, the power of mind that creates the world. Wilbur returns to this subject in "The Terrace," in which a pleasant evening meal on a terrace "High up a mountainside," with a magnificent view, yields this epistemological insight:

And we knew we had eaten not the manna of heaven
But our own reflected light,

And we were the only part of the night that we
Couldn't believe.

This view of a man as creator gives him heroic dimensions, in the fashion of the Elizabethan poets, but
Wilbur, as a twentieth-century poet, is not unaware of
man's roles as killer and victim, and in at least one
poem, "Giacometti," he takes his cue from the Swiss
sculptor and painter to depict man as small, thin, rocky,
and anonymous: "We are this man unspeakably alone/
Yet stripped of the singular utterly, shaved and
scraped/ Of all but being there." Wilbur's ability to
see man in these terms as well as in the positive terms
of creative power points to the range and complexity of
the tensions out of which his poems are made.

In his next book, *Things of This World* (1956),
Wilbur again declares his love of the lights, shadows,
textures, and graces of the world by describing them
with precision. He celebrates the "vague, superb/ And
timeless look" of a black turkey whose "pale-blue bony
head" is "set on its shepherd's crook/ Like a saint's
death-mask." He renders faithfully a scrubwoman who
"flings the scrubwater out, with a crash/ Of grimy rain-
bows, and the stained suds flash/ Like angel-feathers."
He observes and records vividly the summer activity on
the surface of a pond:

Things concentrate at the edges; the pond-surface
Is bourne to fish and man and it is spread

In textile scum and damask light, on which
The lily-pads are set; and there are also
  Inlaid ruddy twigs, becalmed pine-leaves,
  Air-baubles, and the chain mail of froth.

But, as in *Ceremony*, the poet speculates about the reality of this world he renders with such love and precision. Is he dreaming it? Is he alone in space and imagining the properties of reality? Without a man to hear it, will a tree "fall to nothing without a sound"? Describing a misty day in "A Chronic Condition," Wilbur remarks, "Berkeley did not foresee such misty weather," weather that even the imagination cannot penetrate. Over and over again the poet speaks of dreaming, of "dreamt land," of dream-laden reality. And his attitude toward the dream is both positive and negative. It is positive in poems where the imagination serves as a source of value and creative power; it is negative where the dream is delusional, divorced from work and responsibility.

In "Merlin Enthralled," for example, Wilbur asserts that King Arthur needs the magician Merlin, for the man of action always needs the man of imagination to give him dreams and suggest possibilities of glory. Wilbur has Arthur say to Gawen, "Remember when this hand/ Once haled a sword from stone; now no less strong/ It cannot dream of such a thing to do." In the past, it was Merlin who had supplied him with goals

and attitudes. In another poem, "Beasts," Wilbur remarks that the magicians of imagination, the "suitors
of excellence," construe "the painful/ Beauty of
heaven" and make "dreams for men." His praise of the
creative power of the imagination rises to grandeur in
"For the New Railway Station in Rome," which concludes with these lines:

> "What city is eternal
> But that which prints itself within the groping head
> Out of the blue unbroken reveries
> Of the building dead?
>
> "What is our praise or pride
> But to imagine excellence, and try to make it?
> What does it say over the door to heaven
> But *homo fecit?*"

The architecture of heaven itself is the work of the
human imagination.

But Wilbur warns against the force of imagination
that shapes delusion, dream without responsibility, or
illusion that "rides on the whirlpool's rim." It must be
directed, it seems. In the poem entitled "Love Calls Us
to the Things of This World," he describes a man awaking one morning to "a cry of pulleys" as clotheslines
are strung out to dry by invisible women. Half asleep,
he looks out of his window and sees angels instead of
bed sheets and blouses. Pleased with his vision, he

yearns for its continuance and shrinks from reality until
the sun rises and "bitter love" returns him to the things
of this world, where balance is necessary, where subject
and object must coincide:

> Yet, as the sun acknowledges
> With a warm look the world's hunks and colors,
> The soul descends once more in bitter love
> To accept the waking body, saying now
> In a changed voice as the man yawns and rises,
>
> "Bring them down from their ruddy gallows;
> Let there be clean linen for the backs of thieves;
> Let lovers go fresh and sweet to be undone,
> And the heaviest nuns walk in a pure floating
> Of dark habits,
>   keeping their difficult balance."

In 1961, Wilbur published another collection of
poems, *Advice to a Prophet*, in which his epistemological concern is again manifest. What is appearance?
What is reality? When does one become the other?
These questions make for witty paradox, and Wilbur
plays with them engagingly. For example, in "Two
Voices in a Meadow," a milkweed speaks:

> Anonymous as cherubs
> Over the crib of God,
> White seeds are floating
> Out of my burst pod.

What power had I
Before I learned to yield?
Scatter me, great wind:
I shall possess the field.

In other words, to yield is to gain power; to lose is to win. The idea has religious overtones (for hasn't it often been said that he who loses his life gains everlasting life?) and is based on scientific fact: the seeds of the milkweed scatter over a field, take root, and, in a sense, possess it.

The contrast between appearance and reality is at the center of the poem entitled "Junk," in which the objects that are discarded on the junk heaps of contemporary civilization are transformed and given new value. Junk can be "burnt, bulldozed," and then "buried/ To the depths of diamonds, in the making dark." What is ugly and death-dealing—like an ax—can be given a new usefulness and beauty. In the poem "A Summer Morning," Wilbur plays with the idea of true possession: who is the real owner of an estate? The poet seems to agree with the Chinese sage who said that the perceptive seer owns all he sees: the carpenter and cook who enjoy a fine morning on a rich estate possess "what the owner can but own."

When Wilbur turns to the American dream of success, he discovers a dream of failure boring from within. "In the Smoking-Car" is a poem about a tired businessman of the sort who is driven by the need to succeed. He is asleep on a train. Examining the dream behind his eyes, Wilbur discovers a fabulous South Sea island where "the whole air is full of flower-smells" and "Failure, the longed-for valley, takes him in."

In the title poem, "Advice to a Prophet," the poet deals with the prospect of atomic war, stirring the reader to a sense of what such a conflict would mean by presenting images not of a manless world, which is the conventional approach, but of a worldless man. This brilliant paradox suggests the wit of a poet who sees the world as both shadow and substance, subject and object.

But, whatever his doubts about the reality of the world, Wilbur has no doubt about the importance of making a vivid report of its characteristics. Each poem is a carefully articulated structure of sound and sense. The metaphors are exact, making the reality they describe brilliant. For example, here is an image of wind playing in the manes of horses: "That wind's still there that I remember afire/ In the manes of the racing horses/ Veering across the plains." Here is a description of sunlight falling on snow: "the snowfield smarts in the fresh sun,/ And the bells of its melting ring, and we blink/ At the light flexing in trickles." And here is a remarkable impression of a fire truck racing along a street: "Redness, brass, ladders and hats hurl past,/ Blurring to sheer verb."

Richard Wilbur is unquestionably one of the most accomplished of contemporary poets. It can, no doubt, be said that his commitment to traditional techniques is confining; the postulates of the verbal and metrical system that he has adopted rule out a great deal of everyday experience and also the sort of technical experimentation that sees every poem as a challenging new genre. But his excellence, within his limits, is real. His achievement is due to his submission to his art, his craft; it is an effect of will, patience, and love.

W. S. Merwin's subject is the human condition in those aspects that can be called universal. His dramatic change of style in the 1960's, from close metrical structures to open form, should not obscure the fact that he has always been preoccupied with cycles of birth, death, and rebirth. He describes archetypal voyages, journeys, storms, floods, and returns of the prodigal son. When he deals with animals, he gives them an emblematic character reminiscent of the Middle Ages. His first book, *A Mask for Janus,* appeared at the right time, in 1952, when American poets had completed their swing away from war, politics, and economics and were con-

107

centrating on psychological and mythological themes without local or temporal reference. The very title of Mr. Merwin's book suggests his involvement in this trend, for the two-headed god Janus looks backward and forward, toward the past and the future at once, and what he sees is true for all time.

A Mask for Janus contains no specific reference to the America of the 1950's; its stylized landscapes and seas, its archetypal situations, suggest Platonic forms: from these images more specific images are begotten. One seems to be among essences, not among the accidents of time, place, and incarnation. In the poems that deal with Sisyphus, Medusa, and Ulysses, one is presumably in ancient Greece; in the ballad-like poems about palmers and monks one senses a background of medieval Europe; and in other poems one seems to catch glimpses of China and of Palestine in the time of Jesus. But all of these places are idealized, generalized, stripped of identifying particulars. Even the love poems are stylized and formal; in one of them the speaker addresses a mysterious "Lady" whose "intimate subaltern" he wishes to become. In this way distance is achieved—and to maintain it Merwin uses an elevated, mandarin diction and a careful, traditional metric.

The book opens with "Anabasis (I)," a poem which has a closer relationship to Homer's *Odyssey* and Ezra Pound's "Canto I" than to the work by Xenophon from which it takes its title. It is a highly condensed narrative of a voyage over classic seas, told by a member of the crew: one reads about magic islands, bewitched islanders, sirens, and the inevitable descent to the dead. Merwin evokes those primal images of faring forth in a world of mystery and struggle that stir men's dreams, providing the emotional impetus to decision and endeavor. But the poem is not only about a voyage in space, across an imaginary Mediterranean, but also about an expedition in time, from birth to death, from spring to winter. It represents a skillful telescoping of the voyage motif with the seasonal motif of traditional poetry. The first two stanzas suggest the quality of the poem:

> Then we poised, in time's fullness brought
> As to a new country, the senses
> In the mutations of a sallow light,
> A season of signs and speechless;
>
> Thought momently on nothing, knew
> No oratory, no welcome:
> Silence about our silence grew;
> Beached by the convenient stream.

This, obviously, is graceful writing, though the phrase "As to a new country" seems unnecessarily tangential and those "mutations of a sallow light" sound precious.

"Anabasis (II)" is the narrative of another archetypal voyage, recalling, in some details, Rimbaud's "Le

Bateau Ivre." The movement here is not toward old age and death, as it is in "Anabasis (I)," but toward the dissolution of the self in the chaos of sea reality, the anonymity of inorganic matter:

> Fixed to bone only, foreign as we came,
> We float leeward till the mind and body lose
> The uncertain continent of a name.

Another poem with a mythological base is "Dictum: For a Masque of Deluge," in which Merwin tells the story of an apocalyptic flood. It sounds like Noah's experience with wickedness and water, but Merwin carefully generalizes it to include all the other myths of deluge that the imagination of man has created. His is the quintessential flood story: it begins with "the hush of portent," moves on to the fall of torrential rain, the launching of an ark, complete with its pairs of animals, and ends with a recession of waters, the reassertion of land as "the dove/ Makes assignation with the olive tree." It is the old cycle of catastrophe and renewal. It could very well be that, in this poem, Merwin is following the lead of T. S. Eliot, Spengler, and other prophets of doom in predicting the imminent collapse of contemporary civilization, but he obviously does not believe in the finality of any such disaster: there is always a new birth, a new civilization, to replace the old.

Merwin treats these myths with remarkable skill

and smoothness, in traditional metrics and sometimes complicated stanzas. A few of the poems sound like exercises, to be sure—his sonnets, his "half roundel," the two sestinas. The sestina entitled "Variation on a Line by Emerson" is especially awkward; Merwin's extraordinary ingenuity was obviously confounded by the six end words he chose to repeat in this poem. But one can only praise his subtlety of phrase, his admirable impatience with the easy, the merely remembered line, and his succinctness, as in "Epitaph":

> Death is not information.
> Stone that I am,
> He came into my quiet
> And I shall be still for him.

Effects of this sort can be found in Merwin's next book, *The Dancing Bears* (1954), as well. The work reveals the poet's fine control of rhythm and syntax and stirs the reader with verbal surprises, imaginative phrases that are found, on examination, to be amazingly exact. The book is designed like a river: it begins with short trimeter lines in the poem "Tower," establishes a rather thin lyric note, and gradually deepens in voice and mood as the lines lengthen. The last "Canso" is a full-voiced, complexly orchestrated poem that ends on a strong, affirmative note of love.

Like its predecessor, *The Dancing Bears* focuses

on fundamental, recurrent themes of the life of man. For example, "Runes for a Round Table" describes states of being under the influence of Capricorn, Aquarius, Pisces, and the other signs of the zodiac. In "Proteus," which tells of an attempt to seize the wily, shape-changing god of the sea, Merwin says that fixity is impossible: man "battles the foolish shapes/ Of his own death by the insatiate sea." It is a "twice-told tale," to be sure, but Merwin gives it an unusual tilt and a new feeling. He succeeds in doing the same with the old folk tale about the white bear and the peasant maiden in his long narrative poem "East of the Sun and West of the Moon." It is a rich, imaginatively embellished love story the reminds one of the romantic narratives of John Keats. A white bear, really an enchanted prince, woos and wins a peasant girl and carries her off to a magnificent castle that bears a striking resemblance, in its baroque décor, to the mansion in Jean Cocteau's film, *Beauty and the Beast*. Here the girl lives with the white bear, which comes to her at night in the form of a prince. According to the terms of the enchantment, she cannot see his face for a year. She finds this state of affairs unsatisfactory, for she may be sleeping with an ugly man. Expressing a wish to see the woods and meadows of home, where time exists and leaves fall, she pays her mother a visit, plots with her, and then returns to her lover with a candle. She finds that she has been sleeping with a handsome man, but her curiosity ruins the relationship: the prince is compelled to return to his stepmother's palace, which is located east of the sun and west of the moon, and marry another woman. The rest of the poem is taken up with complications in the peasant maiden's search for her lost prince and her ultimate success. The tale is elaborately and charmingly told and serves Merwin as a vehicle for his insights into the complementary nature of the imagination, the moon, and the maiden, on the one hand, and reality, the sun, and the white bear, on the other.

It is clear that the chief distinguishing characteristic of *The Dancing Bears*, as compared with *A Mask for Janus*, is its romanticism, its emphasis on love and the tropes of love. Take, for example, *la belle dame sans merci*. Like Keats, Merwin is fascinated by her. He describes her wittily and gracefully in his poem "The Lady with the Heron." The lady is cruel but beautiful and leads a blind heron about "By the shade of her hand." The speaker loves her, but she is indifferent to him and leaves him unrequited, forlorn: "Blindness I learned/ At the feet of a heron." In another, equally romantic poem, "When I Came From Colchis," the speaker, presumably a Greek who has done battle at Troy, complains that his tough, incredulous neighbors, who had refused to believe his tales of far-off lands and glorious adventures, would never believe the beauty of his love. And in "December: Of Aphrodite" the poet asserts that the goddess of love provides motive power:

"In her name I acted." The book ends with three romantic "Cansos" which, despite rhetorical flourishes that cloud the argument, make clear that the poet puts a tremendous burden on love in what he considers to be a faithless world: "It is by your faith that I believe, I am." And, in return, the poet gives his love immortality, in the way of Shakespeare: "The song is nothing/ If not a resurrection." The best of the three "Cansos" is the last one, in which the poet pictures himself with his love at land's end, listening to the sea:

> We listen, and shall here, love, with the sea's holy
> Song in the shells of our ears, lie down forever
> To sleep in the turning garden for as long as the sea.

It is the lover's acceptance of natural process, change, death, and resurrection, world without end.

Merwin's third book, *Green with Beasts* (1956), represents the climax of the myth-reading phase of his development. Most of the book is committed to the exploration of primal, archetypal, Biblical themes. For example, there is a retelling of the story of the prodigal son, who "went out/ Looking for something his father had not given,/ Delights abroad, some foreign ease, something/ Vague because distant." There is a touching evocation of the grief of the father at the departure of his son and a vivid representation of the shame and contrition of the ruined son as he "takes the first step toward home." In another poem, "The Annunciation," there is a rendering of the thoughts and feelings of the Virgin at the time when she saw an angelic light fill her window with news: with the word for "The way the light and the things in the light/ Were looking into the darkness, and the darkness/ And the things of the darkness were looking into the light." In still another poem, "The Station," the anabasis motif is transformed into a journey of pioneers or immigrants into a wild, new country. They are represented as debating whether to go beyond a shack at a certain way station or return home. Some, indeed, go back, others stay at the station, and a few, not "the bravest/ Or best suited for such a journey," find the energy to "get up and go on" in the morning. The subject provides Merwin with an opportunity to brood over the inscrutability of human motives and capacities.

Part of the book is devoted to descriptions of the character and habits of a select group of animals—a whale, a cockerel, a dog, two horses, a goat, and a ram—which are said to be from "chapters for a bestiary." Another part consists of poems about luckless fishermen and sailors through whose lives the sea reverberates. In one of these poems, drowned sailors watch the keels of ships passing over them and try to recall the stars of their former condition, wondering "how it was that we traced/ In their remote courses not their own fates but ours." But the best of these sea-drenched poems is one entitled "Low Fields and Light," which describes the encroachment of water upon a farm in Virginia:

> My father never plowed there, nor my mother
> Waited, and never knowingly I stood there
> Hearing the seepage slow as growth, nor knew
> When the taste of salt took over the ground.
>
> But you would think the fields were something
> To me, so long I stare out, looking
> For their shapes or shadows through the matted gleam,
>   seeing
> Neither what is nor what was, but the flat light rising.

By 1960, when Merwin's fourth book of poems, *The Drunk in the Furnace*, made its appearance, the tides of American poetry had moved away from mythological and classical analogies and from the rich, complex structures of imagery that the "new critics" had praised and encouraged poets to produce. There were pressures toward free or open forms from poets who wrote projective verse, and there was an emphasis in the magazines on autobiography, family history, and experience for its own sake. Merwin was not insensitive to these forces. *The Drunk in the Furnace* is not without symbols and mythical personages (Odysseus, for instance), but the diction is more colloquial and less rhetorical, and the syntax is simpler. There is much more stress on the senses, as, for example, in "Some Winter Sparrows," a poem made up of vivid, exact images:

> You pursue seeds, wings open on the snow,
>   Coming up then with white
>   Beak, speaking; in my deep foot-prints
>   You vanish, then you flower.

Such details point to the poet's powers of observation and his deep love of reality; these are not merely verbal effects.

One finds many poems about the sea in the new book, as in the preceding ones, and Merwin keeps on reading it for meanings. Among the better ones is "Sailor Ashore," in which he suggests that the land is a sort of ship and that the sea, with its feminine tides, is beneath and around it everywhere; a man's task is to develop sea legs. Another is "Sea Monster," in which a ship's crew think they see a monster and then realize that it is a dream or a trick of the sea. This realization leads them to wonder whether they can ever be sure that they are awake: "we have forgotten/ How it was that, on sea or land, once/ We proved to ourselves that we were awake."

But the chief feature of the book is a section devoted to family history and to people whom Merwin seems to have known: real people, not mythical personages. There is a poem about John Otto, "ancestor/ On my mother's side"; there are others about "Uncle Hess," "Grandfather in the Old Men's Home," "Grandmother Watching at Her Window," and "Grandmother Dying." One reads about a handyman in a summer resort, about men playing pool, and about a drunkard who establishes himself in an old, discarded furnace in a "naked gully." This is subject matter that Merwin had not explored before. There is no doubt that the new autobiographical tide, and particularly the example of Robert Lowell in *Life Studies* and W. D. Snodgrass in *Heart's Needle*, had pushed him in a new direction.

At about the time of the publication of *The Drunk in the Furnace*, Merwin seems to have experienced a crisis not only in subject matter but in style as well, for the poems of the 1960's are astonishingly different from those of the 1950's. There is a point in the career of a poet when he is no longer excited by his own manner; he must change for the sake of his survival as a poet, for the sake of his sense of the truth of things. This seems to have happened to Merwin. At any rate, the style of *The Moving Target* (1963) could not have been predicted on the basis of the four earlier books.

The new book is more colloquial, less mandarin in diction than the preceding ones. In some ways the idiom is antipoetic: there is a deliberate roughening of the line in order to avoid the smoothness, neatness, and sonority of the past. Merwin imitates the awkward phrasing, distorted syntax, and irregular rhythms of the inarticulate: it is a little like the painter Dubuffet imitating the scrawls of children. Merwin abandons traditional metrics grounded in iambic measure for the "open field" versification advocated by Charles Olson. His imagery is fresh, bright, and colorful, like that of such "subjective image" poets as James Wright and Robert Bly. It often depends on the surprise of "happy accidents." The whole effect is somehow tentative, casual: few of the poems are "said" once and for all.

But the themes of *The Moving Target* are not new; they are merely disguised. Merwin's old preoccupation with the anabasis motif, with the classic voyage and the lonely journey on a dangerous road, persists, as does the theme of the return, of the prodigal son come home. One also finds a prophecy of doom for contemporary civilization, as in *A Mask for Janus*: hints of death and resurrection. The difference is that Merwin now seems unwilling to show that he is working with myths; he pretends to be interested in the commonplace realities of the 1960's.

Take, as an example, the theme of the man on the road. In "Air," Merwin describes a man walking and singing on a desert road which has no end, purpose, or meaning beyond seasonal repetition. It is interesting to note that Walt Whitman's open road, by contrast, suggests a future of boundless, rich possibility. Merwin's man forgets the past and the future and concentrates on the present, which he accepts with the amused fortitude of the tramps in Samuel Beckett's *Waiting for Godot:*

> Naturally it is night.
> Under the overturned lute with its
> One string I am going my way
> Which has a strange sound.
>
> This way the dust, that way the dust.
> I listen to both sides
> But I keep right on.
> I remember the leaves sitting in judgment
> And then winter.
>
> I remember the rain with its bundle of roads.
> The rain taking all its roads.
> Nowhere.
>
> Young as I am, old as I am,
>
> I forget tomorrow, the blind man.
> I forget the life among the buried windows.
> The eyes in the curtains.
> The wall
> Growing through the immortelles.
> I forget silence
> The owner of the smile.
>
> This must be what I wanted to be doing,
> Walking at night between the two deserts,
> Singing.

Now, this hero or antihero bears a resemblance to Ishmael, Ulysses, the Wandering Jew, Don Quixote, and

a host of other literary travelers. But Merwin presents
him so casually and with such de-emphasis of personality that he appears to be an anonymous figure of the
1960's; he deliberately rolls away the grand backdrop of
literary tradition that he once painstakingly drew in.

Or consider a poem of departure, of setting sail—
"The Ships Are Made Ready in Silence." It reminds one
of "Anabasis (I)" and "Anabasis (II)" in *A Mask for
Janus:*

> Moored to the same ring:
> The hour, the darkness and I,
> Our compasses hooded like falcons.
>
> Now the memory of you comes aching in
> With a wash of broken bits which never left port,
> In which once we planned voyages.
> They come knocking like hearts asking:
> What departures on this tide?
>
> Breath of land, warm breath,
> You tighten the cold around the navel,
> Though all shores but the first have been foreign,
> And the first was not home until left behind.
>
> Our choice is ours but we have not made it,
> Containing as it does, our destination
> Circled with loss as with coral, and
> A destination only until attained.
>
> I have left you my hope to remember me by,
> Though now there is little resemblance.

At this moment I could believe in no change,
The mast perpetually
Vacillating between the same constellations,
The night never withdrawing its dark virtue
From the harbor shaped as a heart,
The sea pulsing as a heart,
The sky vaulted as a heart,
Where I know the light will shatter like a cry
Above a discovery:
"Emptiness.
Emptiness! Look!"
Look. This is the morning.

The sound of the poem is obviously different from the sound of "Anabasis (I)" or "Anabasis (II)," and its dramatic imagery has the immediacy of real experience; the archetype is well hidden.

The prodigal-son motif has also been transformed in the new book; it is given an American resonance. The son returns to the bosom of his family for Thanksgiving after a period of empty, cold wandering down the roads of the world. He describes his experiences as follows in "Home for Thanksgiving":

Well this is nice with my shoes moored by the bed
And the lights around the bill-board ticking on and
    off like a beacon,
I have brought myself back like many another crusty
Unbarbered vessel launched with a bottle,
From the bare regions of pure hope where

For a great part of the year it scarcely sets at all,
And from the night skies regularly filled with old
      movies of my fingers,
Weightless as shadows, groping in the sluices,
And from the visions of veins like arteries, and
From the months of plying
Between can and can, vacant as a pint in the morning,
While my sex grew into the only tree, a joyless
      evergreen,
And the winds played hell with it at night, coming as
      they did
Over at least one thousand miles of emptiness,
Thumping as though there were nothing but doors,
      insisting
"Come out," and of course I would have frozen.

This is, clearly, a despairing view of an inhospitable world in which only family relationships are capable of generating a measure of warmth. But the book does not end on this note. As in his other works, Merwin looks beyond the catastrophes of modern history, beyond injustice and greed, to the cyclical renewals to come. Characterizing the people of Manhattan as "Prisoners in the watch towers," he remarks: "The mouse bones in the plaster/ Prepare for the resurrection." The book ends with a poem entitled "Daybreak" in which the poet says, "An open doorway/ Speaks for me/ Again."

As is evident from the work of the poets already considered, mythological and psychological archetypes constituted the themes of a great deal of American poetry in the early 1950's. The universality of this subject matter, with its register of echoes from many centuries, made possible the aesthetic distance and "anonymity" that "new critics" like John Crowe Ransom prized. It also made possible a concentration on technique, on such elements as irony, paradox, richness of texture, and complexity of rhythmic structure. But widespread dissatisfaction with "academic" poetry, which was con-

124

sidered to be out of touch with the realities of life, moved a group of poets associated with Charles Olson, who was at that time on the staff of Black Mountain College, to strike out in another direction.

Like Whitman, who invited the muses of Greece to migrate to America, these poets insisted on a poetry rooted in American experience, phrased in a contemporary American idiom, and organized to reflect the rhythms of ordinary American speech. This program, strongly reminiscent of the literary nationalism of the 1850's, drew the support of Robert Duncan and Robert Creeley, both of whom, like Olson, were on the faculty of Black Mountain College, and of such other contemporaries as Paul Blackburn and Denise Levertov. They found a publishing outlet in Cid Corman's *Origin*, a journal that went through twenty issues between 1951 and 1956, and later in the *Black Mountain Review*, which lasted for seven issues, from 1954 to 1957. In time such magazines as *Big Table, Yugen,* and *Evergreen Review* published the poets of the new cause. The poets who appeared in these magazines either knew one another personally or kept in touch by letter (some of them had corresponded with Ezra Pound and William Carlos Williams) and so developed the tenets of their movement. Paul Blackburn said in an article in *Kulchur 10* that he had met Robert Creeley through Ezra Pound: "We had already been in touch through EP's good services—Pound in St. Elizabeth's was a very valuable clearing house for putting the young in touch with one another."

The key difference between the poets associated with Charles Olson and the traditionalists is to be found in their conception of rhythms and forms appropriate to American space, time, and experience.

The poets of long memory, responsive to the rhythms of the great accentual-syllabic poetry of England that dates back to Chaucer, deny, of course, that the English language as it is spoken in America is so markedly different from the English spoken in England that poets must abandon the metrics that organized poetry in the past. No matter where it is spoken, English is a strongly accented language unlike, say, French, in which there is an even distribution of stresses, and poets usually take this fact into account when building structures of rhythm. The basic unit of traditional English meter is the iambic foot, that is, an unaccented syllable followed by an accented one, and a pattern of such feet provides a rhythmic pulse against which variations in the number and placement of accented and unaccented syllables can play. Together with pauses in the middle of lines, these variations make possible an astonishing range and subtlety of sound and feeling, and they can embody a counterpoint of conversational cadences in play with a pattern of rhythmic expectations.

That it is possible to suggest the cadences of American speech while retaining the rhythmic pulse of iambic measure is clear from the work of Robert Frost, who once remarked, in defending his practice, that writing free verse is like playing tennis with the net down. Here, for example, are the opening lines of "An Old Man's Winter Night":

> All out-of-doors looked darkly in at him
> Through the thin frost, almost in separate stars,
> That gathers on the pane in empty rooms.
> What kept his eyes from giving back the gaze
> Was the lamp tilted near them in his hand.
> What kept him from remembering what it was
> That brought him to that creaking room was age.
> He stood with barrels round him—at a loss.

The colloquial diction of this passage ("All out-of-doors," "What kept him," and "at a loss"), the straight-forward syntax (no inversions of subject and predicate), and the roll of phrases in units of attention that can be managed easily in oral delivery (the first line, for example, runs on to a strong caesura in the middle of the second line) identify it as Frost's work and as American speech. But it is held together by a rhythmic frame that can be found in Shakespeare's plays also. The units of oral delivery play against this blank-verse net, which obviously does not hamper Frost in the least and makes possible tremendous emphasis at points where meaning stress and meter stress correspond, as, for example, in the words "frost," "lamp," "age," and "loss." Frost achieves additional rhythm through the repetition of the "what" clauses in lines 4 and 6, and he avoids monotony by the use of substitute feet (two spondees in the first line, a pyrrhic followed by a spondee in lines 2 and 5, and an anapaest in line 6).

Among recent poets who have written new and recognizably "American" poems in traditional rhythm one can mention Robert Lowell, Richard Wilbur, W. D. Snodgrass, Jean Garrigue, and Howard Nemerov. Many of them have also written free verse.

But Charles Olson, speaking for his associates, wants American poetry "to go ahead," to reject the artifice of traditional measure in favor of what he calls Field Composition or Projective Verse. He has learned from Ezra Pound to "compose in the sequence of the musical phrase, not in the sequence of the metronome," and from William Carlos Williams to write lines of verse in units of attention or "variable feet."

Olson's essential point is that the function of a poem, which he defines as "a high-energy-construct," is to transfer energy or life force from the poet to the reader and that the best way to make this transfer is by means of open or field composition, not by writing "closed" verse, by which Olson means all metered poetry. In this view, "Form is never more than an extension of content," and field composition involves a steady, dense stream of perceptions: "One perception must immediately and directly lead to a further perception." In this view, also, the sound of syllables as they unroll from the mind, one by one, makes for the harmony of the poem. The lines that give it shape on the page spring from the breath of the poet: "the line comes (I swear it) from the breath, from the breathing of the man who writes, at the moment that he writes, and thus is, it is here that, the daily work, the WORK, gets in, for only he, the man who writes, can declare, at every moment, the line its metric and its ending—where its breathing, shall come to, termination." Since he can produce lines of varying length and novel arrangements of print on the page, the poet working in open-field composition has a chance "to indicate exactly the breath, the pauses, the suspensions even of syllables, the juxtapositions even of parts of phrases, which he intends." Because of his stress on auditory effects, Olson neglects to note that projective verse could also, at least in theory, produce visual rhythms and harmonies in the fashion of E. E. Cummings: leaps and plays of eye that print makes possible.

Olson nowhere says why the poet or his reader cannot breathe whenever he wishes, without waiting for the end of a line. And, in general, he tends to neglect those aspects of poetry that are not related to voice and breath. It can be argued, for instance, that poetry is a constellation of meanings and images in an ideographic sense, that its appearance in print, on a page,

where the eye can retrace its course, makes it vastly
different from oral communication.

Here, at any rate, is an example of projective verse
from "The Songs of Maximus," by Charles Olson:

This morning of the small snow
I count the blessings, the leak in the faucet
which makes of the sink time, the drop
of the water on water as sweet
as the Seth Thomas
in the old kitchen
my father stood in his drawers to wind (always
he forgot the 30th day, as I don't want to remember
the rent
    a house these days
so much somebody else's,
especially,
Congoleum's

    Or the plumbing,
that it doesn't work, this I like, have even used paper clips
as well as string to hold the ball up   And flush it
with my hand
    But that the car doesn't, that no moving thing moves
without that song I'd void my ear of, the musicracket
of all ownership . . .
    Holes
in my shoes, that's all right, my fly
gaping, me out
at the elbows, the blessing
    that difficulties are once more

"In the midst of plenty, walk
as close to
bare
    In the face of sweetness,
piss
      In the time of goodness,
go side, go
smashing, beat them, go as
 (as near as you can

tear

In the land of plenty, have
nothing to do with it
          take the way of
the lowest,
including your legs, go
contrary, go

sing

This interesting poem sounds new, clearly, but not much newer than the work of Ezra Pound or William Carlos Williams. It has Williams' preoccupation with humble detail and Pound's belligerent, anti-bourgeois stance in support of the artist. Moreover, it has Pound's and T. S. Eliot's allusiveness, for there is a reference in it to the Elizabethan lyric "Back and Side, Go Bare, Go Bare." In form it is open, as theory requires, and perception follows perception as the poet's mind examines the coercions of circumstance. Olson widens and narrows his units of attention, his line lengths, dropping suddenly from line to line for emphasis, enacting the "I" character's stubborn response to reality. It is a spirited poem, deliberate even in its casualness—in, for example, Olson's failure to close his quotation and his parentheses.

Olson's projective verse has animated the poetic practice of Robert Duncan, Denise Levertov, Robert Creeley, and Paul Blackburn, and it has either influenced or coincided with other stirrings toward newness in American poetry. It goes along with the highly repetitive, free-form verse of Lawrence Ferlinghetti and Ted Joans, meant for recital to jazz accompaniment, and with the new spontaneous poetry of total response. Olson's breath-conditioned lines have encouraged a mystique of physiological process, according to which the poem is a reflection of the pulse of the poet's life, and the less interference there is from the censors of consciousness, with their rational controls, the better. This is not a negation of form, it seems, but a redefinition of it. A tree achieves its form through an adjustment of internal reality to external circumstance, as it rises through air to branches and twigs; the human body develops similarly: it is not stamped out in a machine press like fenders or wheels. The poem with an organic shape reflects the living poet, just as the poet, in turn, is said to reflect another artist, God. In *Ion*, Plato remarks that God takes away the minds of poets in order to speak through them. Some of the more mystic poets, feeling that they are the reeds of a rather latitudinarian God, strain mightily to express their lives freely and fully. Allen Ginsberg puts the case in this way:

> Trouble with conventional form (fixed line count & stanza form) is, it's too symmetrical, geometrical, numbered and prefixed—unlike to my own mind which has no beginning and end, nor fixed measure of thought (or speech—or writing) other than its own cornerless mystery—to transcribe the latter in a form most nearly representing its actual "occurrence" is my "method"— which requires the Skill of freedom of composition— and which will lead Poetry to the expression of the highest moments of the mindbody—mystical illumination—and its deepest emotion (through tears—love's all)—in the form nearest to what it actually looks like (data of mystical imagery) & feels like (rhythm of actual speech & rhythm prompted by direct transcription of visual & other mental data)—plus not to forget the sudden genius-like Imagination or fabulation of unreal & out of this world verbal constructions which express the true gaiety & excess of Freedom—(and also by their nature express the First Cause of the world) by means of spontaneous irrational juxtaposition of sublimely related fact, . . .

In order to reach irrational or suprarational states of God-intoxication, in which the composition of a poem could be said to be spontaneous and true, some of the poets encourage whatever tendencies they may have toward hallucination; they experiment with vision-producing drugs such as peyote, mescaline, ayahuasca, and marijuana. Others make a study of Zen Buddhism, delighted by its mind-shattering conundrums, its aim to disturb the consciousness into a keen perception of the present, moment by moment, as it is lived. Their aesthetic of spontaneity derives, in part, from a Zen-conditioned Japanese art, Sumiye ink-sketching, which is done without conscious control or correction. Each sketch is indelible and irrevocable, like a man's life. D. T. Suzuki, the noted exponent of Zen Buddhism, describes the technique as follows:

> The artist must follow his inspiration as spontaneously and absolutely and instantly as it moves; he just lets his arm, his fingers, his brush be guided by it as if they were all mere instruments, together with his whole being, in the hands of somebody else who has temporarily taken possession of him. Or we may say that the brush by itself executes the work quite outside the artist, who just lets it move on without his conscious efforts. If any logic or reflection comes between brush and paper, the whole effect is spoiled. In this way Sumiye is produced.

And in this way a great deal of contemporary poetry is being produced. As Michael McClure says, "I write and make no/or few changes. The prime purpose of my writing is liberation." This way of writing does, indeed, lead to the discovery of "alluvials," as Jack Kerouac calls them, but it rarely produces a formally complete poem. When it does, the poem is a miracle, a "happy accident."

This approach has affinities with theories of organic form held by the Transcendentalists of the nineteenth century, particularly Ralph Waldo Emerson, and with the practice of Walt Whitman, who in the 1855 preface to *Leaves of Grass* said that "The rhyme and uniformity of perfect poems show the free growth of metrical laws and bud from them as unerringly and loosely as lilacs or roses on a bush, and take shapes as compact as the shapes of chestnuts and oranges and melons and pears, and shed the perfume impalpable to form." It also has affinities with the automatic-writing experiments of Gertrude Stein and the Dadaists of the First World War and with the work of French Surrealists of the 1920's and 1930's. But several of the poets trace their inspiration to the nonobjective "action" painting of Jackson Pollock and the New York School of the 1950's, among them such poets as John Ashbery, Kenneth Koch, and Frank O'Hara.

In practice, the poets of the new orientation have succeeded in writing verse that is close to the speech rhythms of contemporary America. In their admission of "antipoetic" materials they have also widened the scope of poetry. But, since the composition of good verse without the aid of traditional metrical structures requires a fine ear—and a fine ear is a rarity—much projective verse is dull, diffuse, and sub-literary in quality. Much of it is also opaque, devoid of imagery. It lacks the rich textures that rhyme, assonance, and alliteration make possible in closed rhythmic structures. However, the work of Robert Duncan, Denise Levertov, and Robert Creeley is outstanding.

(a)   Charles Olson

The views of Charles Olson as theoretician of Open Field Composition may be found in his essay "Projective Verse," which was printed in *Poetry New York*, No. 3 (1950), pp. 13–22. His poems may be examined in the following broadsides, pamphlets, and books: *Y & X* (1948), *Letter for Melville 1951* (1951), *This* (1952), *The Maximus Poems 1–10* (1953), *Anecdotes of the Late War* (1955), *The Maximus Poems 11–22* (1956), *O'Ryan 246810* (1958), *The Maximus Poems* (1960), *The Distances* (1960), and *Maximus, from Dogtown—I* (1961).

All of Olson's poems are written in "breath-conditioned" lines, in accordance with his theories, and their themes are on such matters as the rise and fall of civilizations (Olson is an archaeologist and student of ancient history), the health of the good society threatened by "pejorocracy," and the value of good writing as an index to the life and moral condition of a people.

Even as far back as 1948, when he published a pamphlet of five open-form poems entitled *Y & X*, Olson struck characteristic notes. In one poem, for example, he reconciles himself to the thought that he will not be alive in the year 2000 by de-emphasizing individual death: "Is it of such concern when what shall be/ already is within the moonward sea?" He sees nature moving in cycles, coming back "Full circle," for "The salts and minerals of the earth return." And in another poem, "La Préface," Olson takes up his lifelong battle against "closed form," in this case by attacking the closed parenthesis: "The closed parenthesis reads: the dead bury the dead,/ and it is not very interesting."

Letter for Melville 1951 was inspired by the Melville Society's "One Hundredth Birthday Party" for *Moby-Dick* at Williams College. Olson rages at the professors of American literature who took part in this celebration, accusing them of commercialism and academic careerism, of advancing themselves by grinding out books about the great man. There is no excuse, he thunders, "for this abomination, for the false & dirty thing which it is—nothing more than a bunch of commercial travellers from the several colleges." Having himself lived in close association with the academic community (at Clark, Harvard, and Black Mountain

College), Olson is particularly sensitive to the politics of status-seeking in intellectual circles, where it does not belong, and, having himself written a book about Herman Melville (*Call Me Ishmael*, 1947), he is eager to separate from a corrupt academic community an author who had found his Yale and Harvard aboard a whaling ship.

Olson's broadside *This* (1952) contributes to the popular mystique of the bullfight. The poet finds ontological meaning in the action in the arena; he sees the encounter with the bull as "this/ instant declaration of that which you know is all/ that constitutes both what you are and what is going on at all time." But this is not to say that Olson likes violence. As a matter of fact, he is consistently opposed to war. His broadside *Anecdotes of the Late War* (1955) is an antiwar document relating to the Civil War. His point is powerfully made: "better, that is, that a man stay lethargic than/ blow somebody's face off—off,/ the face of, blow/ the earth." Elsewhere Olson remarks:

What he said was, in that instance
I got there first
with the most men

Grant didn't hurry.
He just had the most.

More of the latter died.

A much less serious work appeared in 1958, *O'Ryan 246810,* which describes the plight of a rough-and-ready character named O'Ryan who has been thrown over by his girl and is, in consequence, "all white/ and looking all over."

A more considerable achievement than these pamphlets and broadsides is *The Maximus Poems,* on which Olson has been engaged for many years. Sections of this work were published in 1953, 1956, 1960, and 1961. The 1960 edition contains the two earlier volumes and a sheaf of new poems. The work that came out in 1961, *Maximus, from Dogtown—I,* is a pamphlet containing a single poem about a handsome sailor named Merry who made a practice of wrestling publicly with a bull calf in order to exhibit his prowess. When the calf grew up, he stopped wrestling with it. Then, forced by public opinion to renew the match, he took on the grown bull and lost his life: the bull tore him to pieces. This is one of the more arresting Maximus poems, with its vivid action and ironic implications about the relationship between genius, pride, public opinion, and insuperable natural force.

Most of the other Maximus poems contain far less drama and crystallized meaning of the sort that an object or an action can carry implicitly. They are, in fact, discursive, fragmentary, and antipoetic in the sense that they contain propositions and notes for poems without much rendering, ordering, or assimilation. As there is no narrative thread, continuity is provided by a recurrence of themes and the presence of a stable center of consciousness, the poet's. The poet is the hero of the poem, as he is in Ezra Pound's *Cantos* and William Carlos Williams' *Paterson*. His values dominate the scene as he observes and examines. Olson's scene is Gloucester, Massachusetts, his home town, and it is his embattled spirit, commenting on the life and history of the place, that gives motion and emotion to *The Maximus Poems*. Many of the poems are called letters, and they are addressed to the citizenry of Gloucester, praising their labor and warning them against the folly of commitment to the more specious values of contemporary industry and commerce. He attacks the cheapness, superficiality, and standardization that he sees everywhere and asks his townspeople to search for lasting values:

> But that which matters, that which insists, that which will
> last,
> that! o my people, where shall you find it, how, where, where
> shall you listen
> when all is become billboards, when, all even silence, is
> spray-gunned?

This is, clearly, an instance of "pejorocracy," a term that is as central to *The Maximus Poems* as *usura* is to Pound's *Cantos*. But it should be noted that Olson has none of Pound's aristocratic bias; the degradation he inveighs against is not a consequence of the spread of power to the people but of the seemingly calculated attempt of manufacturers to transform the American people into a mass of consumers. To the advertiser's view of America, Olson opposes an appealing New England individualism:

There are no hierarchies, no infinite, no such many as mass,
        there are only
eyes in all heads,
to be looked out of

He stresses the heterogeneity of Gloucester:

As the people of the earth are now, Gloucester
is heterogeneous, and so can know polis
not as localism, not that mu-sick (the trick
of corporations, newspapers, slick magazines, movie
        houses,
the ships, even the wharves, absentee-owned

they whine to my people, these entertainers, sellers

they play upon their bigotries (upon their fears

He likes the variety and distinction that he finds among his townspeople. He likes, for instance, the gentle land-lord who is so sensitive that he cannot ask his tenants for rent. He reaches out to him and to all "Isolatos" (Melville's term for the crew of the "Pequod"), hoping to communicate some human warmth.

He also hopes to communicate a sense of the value of being, of living, of engaging in primary activities that are an end in themselves. He describes a "flowering plum/ out the front door window" which "sends whiteness" inside his house and observes that

> there is no other issue than
> the moment of
> > the pleasure of
> > > this plum,
>
> these things
> which don't carry their end any further than
> their reality in
> themselves

He thinks his townspeople are prevented from seeing this reality by the pejorocracy of profiteers who have dominated New England history and have encouraged a belief in the supreme value of material possessions. Speaking of a New England financier, he says:

> He represents, then, the movement of NE monies
> away from primary production & trade
> to the several cankers of profit-making
> which have, like Agyasta, made America great.

Meantime, of course, swallowing up
the land and labor. And now,
the world.

The work of the financial operator is, in his view, related to the politics of the "culture monger" and the irresponsible phrasemaker who specializes in euphemisms and prevents the townspeople from recognizing the truth:

Let those who use words cheap, who use us cheap
take themselves out of the way
Let them not talk of what is good for the city

The Maximus Poems clearly reflects Olson's grass-roots radicalism and humanism, which provide the emotional charge for much of the book. The work belongs to the great tradition of long poems of epic intent, of noble voice, in which the theme is of national scope: the founding of a state and the ordering of a good society. Since Olson's politics is not narrowly programmatic, the book escapes the rigidity that often mars works of dogma and persuasion. If anything, it needs a measure of dogma; dogma might have helped the poet to achieve a structure. As it stands, the book is shapeless. It has neither beginning nor end; it is all middle. It reminds one of wallpaper rather than of a formally complete, framed picture. One assumes that Olson intended this effect, as corresponding to his sense of reality.

The Distances (1960) contains most of Olson's poems that do not belong to the Maximus complex. Here one finds two of the poems that had appeared earlier as broadsides: *Letter for Melville 1951* and *Anecdotes of the Late War*. And here one comes upon several impressive poems like "The Kingfishers." Here Olson looks at change in terms of such propositions as "What does not change/ is the will to change" and "Into the same river no man steps twice" and "Around an appearance, one common model, we grow up." He also moves ambitiously into the matter of the decline of civilizations, change as decay, attributing it in part to the corruptions of pejorocracy, which makes for an environment "where dirtiness is law." But Olson's most brilliant comment on the destruction of a civilization appears in the lines that evoke Angkor, perhaps: "When the attentions change/ the jungle/ leaps in/ even the stones are split." It is very persuasive, that clause: "When the attentions change."

Among the other notable poems in the collection are "There Was a Youth Whose Name Was Thomas Granger," which tells about an incontinent young man who was executed for bestiality in early New England; "The Lordly and Isolate Satyrs," which describes a group of handsome, androgynous muscle men on a beach; and "Variations Done for Gerald Van de Wiele," which is a lively, lyrical description of a morning in spring.

Any student of the work of Charles Olson is bound to come away with respect and admiration for his humanity and his sense of the importance of the workshop and all elemental activity. But, because much of his work is fragmentary and has the character of notes for poems, jottings, "pre-poetry," it rarely provides a sustained experience of either language or reality.

(b) Robert Duncan

Robert Duncan is a poet of cosmic consciousness whose mystical raptures transport him into areas of spirit where the Many are One, where all forms have their Original Being, and where eternal Love encompasses all reality, both Good and Evil. As a visionary, he has a bridgebuilding, time-binding, and space-binding imagination. He speaks of a meadow which is like

> a scene made-up by the mind
> that is not mine, but is a made place,
>
> that is mine, it is so near to the heart,
> an eternal pasture folded in all thought
> so that there is a hall therein
>
> that is a made place, created by light
> wherefrom the shadows that are forms fall.

It is this "light" from which all forms fall that is at the center of his universe, his God, and it is there that all life returns, as the "Pasture" section of "Four Pictures of the Real Universe" makes clear:

> The Great Sun Himself comes
> to eat at my heart, asks
> that I return myself into Him.
>
> And the white body, a Moon,
> in the precincts of the Earth revolves.
> How the Dead draw the Sea after them!
>
> But the Living, the immortal corpuscles
> sail without shadow
> toward the pyres of the Sun.

A similar sense of the systole-diastole of the cosmic heart, the expansion and contraction of all creation under the Sun, can be found in Duncan's "The Ballad of the Enamord Mage":

> How the Earth turns round under the Sun I know,
> And how the Numbers in the Constellations glow,
> How all Forms in Time will grow
> And return to their single Source
> Informed by Grief, Joy, insatiable Desire
> And cold Remorse.

This Sun, this God, of the poet is sometimes equated with Love—a merciful and boundless Love.

That God should be Love seems absolutely necessary to Duncan's imagination, perhaps because of his horror of appearances and his need for an ultimate positivism. As he remarks in his *Letters* (1958), "all conviction of atheism disappears before the liberation in which there are only loves equal before God. For this God in which we dwell finds all our loves as we knew them to be: the Love."

Fortified by this vision of ultimate Love, Duncan can face and endure the contradictions, delusions, and evils of the world. It is not surprising that he sometimes sees his experience in terms of crucifixion. Even as early as the "Treesbank Poems" of his first book, *Heavenly City, Earthly City* (1947), Duncan identifies with Christ:

> Glad Christ! of whom partaking I
> am—as a universe is crucified in me—
> Christ-crossed upon the body of my world.

The terrors and tortures of the world are part of a universal process. "Death is prerequisite to the growth of grass," the poet says in a poem entitled "Nor Is the Past Pure," where he also declares that

> Thus the Evil is seed, terror
>   held by courage (our labors) nourishd
> by devotion (our labors)
>   anticipates Beauty.

This view of evil can also be found in "This Place Rumord to Have Been Sodom," where Duncan says that "The world like Great Sodom lies under love/ and knows not the hand of the Lord that moves." This hand has measured Sodom and found it wanting, but it is not the cruel, punishing hand of a despot. The Lord, after all, is Love, and the poem ends on this note: "This place rumord to have been Sodom is blessd/ in the Lord's eyes."

This God of light and love is one of Duncan's three major subjects, the other two being the imagination and poetry. Sometimes the three are bound in so close a relationship that they seem interchangeable: aspects of the same reality. There is a touch of Wallace Stevens in Duncan's easy transitions from the subjective to the objective, in making God an expression of the poet's imagination in some contexts, and, in others, the poet's maker. Consider, for example, the following statement: "If one views all religions as human inventions, projections and pageants of the imagination, then Christ may be included, adored; one may even, seeking salvation there, come into heaven without casting a world into hell." This observation is interesting partly because it reveals Duncan's commitment to the God of Love— to salvation without hell—but chiefly because it suggests that the human imagination is supreme as creator and value-giver: all religions are constructs of the imagination, just as the colors and shapes of the world are.

Duncan's preoccupation with the imagination was evident even as far back as 1950, when he published *Medieval Scenes*, a book in which "the poet" appears in various disguises: as David fighting Goliath, as a weaver of tapestries, as a lover, *et al.* Two years later Duncan issued a broadside entitled *Song of the Borderguard* in which he depicts the poet as a guard on the frontiers of language: "The borderlines of sense in the morning light/ are naked as a line of poetry in a war." He pursues the same theme in *Letters* (1958) and in *The Opening of the Field* (1960), especially in the latter work, which contains thirteen poems entitled "The Structure of Rime" and several others on related subjects, among them "Poetry, a Natural Thing" and "Keeping the Rhyme." In all of these poems the world of natural objects (alive and holy because God is immanent), the imagination, and language breathe as one. At one point Duncan says, "There is a woman who resembles the sentence." Elsewhere he says, "The eyes that are horns of the moon feast on the leaves of trampled sentences." In another poem he says, "The Master of Rime, time after time, came down the arranged ladders of vision or ascended the smoke and flame towers of the opposite of vision, into or out of the language of daily life, husband to one word, wife to the other, breath that leaps forward upon the edge of dying." It is a vision of divine, imaginative union that Duncan is offering here; reading his poems is like walking through a brilliant, subjective landscape. "As we start the sentence," Duncan remarks, "we notice that birds are flying thru it."

Early and late in his career, Duncan has been writing in the free forms of projective verse. His practice can be summarized in his own phrase: "a loosening of conventions and return to open form." He works in the rhythms of ordinary American speech, and he shapes his lines irregularly, to accord with leaps and changes of feeling and thought. He prefers a rugged directness of phrase to mellifluousness of line or eloquence. He is capable of embarrassing awkwardness—some passages are so crabbed and ill-phrased that they are unspeakable—but this awkwardness is often intended—as part of his effort to escape tradition. In "For a Muse Meant" he says, "A great effort, straining, breaking up/ all the melodic line (the lyr-/ ick strain?) Dont/ hand me that old line we say/ You dont know what yer saying." Elsewhere, in *Letters*, he says, "I attempt the discontinuities of poetry. To interrupt all sure course of my inspiration." He is obviously interested in honest statement and aims to achieve it by avoiding all easy rhythms and all the seductions of the expected.

Robert Duncan has published the following books: *Heavenly City, Earthly City* (1947), *Poems, 1948–*

1949 (1949), *Medieval Scenes* (1950), *Song of the Borderguard* (1952), *Fragments of a Disordered Devotion* (1952), *Caesar's Gate* (1955), *Letters* (1958), *Selected Poems* (1959), *The Opening of the Field* (1960), and *Roots and Branches* (1964).

(c) Robert Creeley

Of all the poets associated with Charles Olson in the projective-verse movement, Robert Creeley is the most laconic, bare, and tangential in phrasing, the least interested in rendering, dramatizing, and persuading. He has no opulence or bravura, no interest in magic. He is, in fact, parsimonious; words leave his pocket one by one, like hard-earned pennies. In theory he is committed to "open form" composition; like Olson, he speaks of "lines/ talking, taking, always the beat from/ the breath." But in practice he produces tight, short, carefully controlled poems that seem "closed" except for the absence of rhyme and meter.

Here is "I Know a Man," a characteristic Creeley poem:

As I sd to my
friend, because I am
always talking,—John, I

sd, which was not his
name, the darkness sur-
rounds us, what

can we do against
it, or else, shall we &
why not, buy a goddamn big car,

drive, he sd, for
christ's sake, look
out where yr going.

Like most Creeley poems, this one has the syntax, phrasing, and rhythm of ordinary speech; it lacks imagery;
and it presents honestly, with a touch of humor, a very
human foible and predicament. The speaker and the
reader are jolted into a suddenly widening awareness of
the dangers of the world. The spare, tight form here is
not a strait jacket but neatly contains Creeley's vision
of a man philosophizing grandly about the darkness that
surrounds him even as he moves in a materialistic dream
of possessing "a goddamn big car," a dream from which
he is aroused by a companion with a mole-like sense of
the immediate reality, the possibility of cracking up.
The speaker is obviously high, for he can't remember
his friend's name. The seemingly casual, offhand col-
location of incongruities in the poem makes for great
impact when the particulars are seen to be related. This
is Creeley at his best.

Creeley published seven slim volumes of poetry during the 1950's which found their way to a small but enthusiastic audience. These were *Le Fou* (1952), *The Immoral Proposition* (1953), *The Kind of Act of* (1953), *All That Is Lovely in Men* (1955), *If You* (1956), *The Whip* (1957), and *A Form of Women* (1959). Most of the poems in these books were later collected in *For Love, Poems 1950–1960* (1962).

His major subject is love, or, rather, the transformations of love that occur as a man moves from courtship to marriage, responsibility, habit, and fatherhood. His poems describe the transports, disenchantments, crises of trust, hopes, and despairs of the love relationship, which is often made to bear a greater weight than it is capable of bearing. As Creeley says in "Song," "But fate, love, fate/ scares me. What/ I took in my hand/ grows in weight." Accused of pedestrianism and narrowness of subject matter, Creeley once said, "I have been called a 'domestic' poet, which celebration Robert Graves somewhere suggests is the death of the Muse altogether. But such is my 'world,' like they say—what space I can recognize—and with no confinement of anything whatsoever. At one time, it must have been, a woman was this insistence, i.e., a fact in herself so variable her very presence was a wonder. Well, now where is she? I think I have been there now and again,—simply there. A poet, call him what you will, knows his

Muse, 'domestic drudge' or not. To hell with it. Let each man save himself as best he can."

Sometimes, upset by some misunderstanding, Creeley wants to sever all human relationships and withdraw. In "The Immoral Proposition," for example, he considers that "If you never do anything for anyone else/ you are spared the tragedy of human relation-/ ships." And in poem after poem he points out the inadequacies and ego-shattering cruelties and guilts of the closest human ties. In "Ballad of the Despairing Husband" he describes rather humorously a marriage which could be characterized in one brief line: "I fought with her, she fought with me." In another poem, "The Gift," the speaker offers his lady "his/ precious/ understanding clothed/ in miraculous/ fortitude," and she fails to see its value and cries out petulantly, "is/ that all, is/ that all." Sometimes it is a trivial matter that brings on a crisis: "Let me say (in anger) that since the day we were married/ we have never had a towel/ where anyone could find it,/ the fact." Sometimes it is a fear of deception: "If you love/ her how prove she/ loves also, except that it/ occurs, a remote chance on/ which you stake/ yourself?"

But there is another room in every love relationship, and it is for the sake of occasional residence there that the poet risks his life. In "The Rhyme," Creeley says:

I saw her
and behind her there were
flowers, and behind them
nothing.

Many of Creeley's poems are ironic and wryly humorous, whether they deal with love or some other experience. The whole point of "The Ball Game," for example, lies in an ironic mischance: "The one damn time (7th inning)/ standing up to get a hot dog someone spills/ mustard all over me." Creeley is amused by the human comedy in a poem called "After Lorca":

The church is a business, and the rich
are the business men.
    When they pull on the bells, the
poor come piling in and when a poor man dies, he has a
  wooden
cross, and they rush through the ceremony.

But when a rich man dies, they
drag out the Sacrament
and a golden Cross, and go *doucement, doucement*
to the cemetery.

And the poor love it
and think its crazy.

The conventional contrast between the rich and the poor (the province of social reformers) is here transformed by the perception at the end: the poor folk "love" the spectacle!

In all these poems Creeley's purpose is not so much to render an experience as to define it for himself and for a hypothetical audience as alert to incongruity as he is. As he himself says, "The process of definition is the intent of the poem." In defining the areas of experience that trouble him, Creeley relies heavily on cognition and neglects the senses. He seems to dislike description. He says, "*Description* does nothing, it includes the object,—it neither hates nor loves." Now, it is true that a poem must have emotion to achieve any sort of animation, but it cannot dispense with objects that arouse the requisite emotion. It is only by means of objects that a poem can give its readers an illusion of experience.

It is interesting to note that Creeley is not indifferent to description in his fiction. His first novel, *The Island* (1963), is like a gloss on his poems, for it elaborates on his favorite theme, love in marriage. It is essentially the story of a young American writer and his wife during a stay on the literary island of Mallorca. Here the writer is seen in the company of an English friend, a French artist, a poet from Liverpool, visitors from Australia, and several tourists. The focus is on his relationship with his wife: on their bickering, fumbled love-making, and gradual estrangement. The novel is carefully understated but vivid in its similes—a love relationship, for example, is compared to "a process like that of decompression, for the diver." Creeley's chief virtue as a novelist is his ability to tell a terrible story of marital misunderstanding without melodrama or contrived incident: he allows his characters and events to develop naturally, slowly, with due regard for the accidental and imponderable. And what he has to say is true enough: that even the closest human relationships are soaked in guilt from which one must recover as well as one can, with or without dignity.

(d)   Denise Levertov

There is no doubt that association with Charles Olson, Robert Duncan, and Robert Creeley in their projective-verse experiments has contributed significantly to the development of Denise Levertov as a poet, enabling her to achieve an individuality of style and voice that was wholly absent from her early work. She began by writing poems in the traditional accentual-syllabic metrics of English poetry, but she was not conspicuously successful in making her own voice heard above those of countless other poets who had worked in the same tradition. The metrical and stanzaic patterns and rhyme schemes to which she committed herself in her first book, *The Double Image* (1946), were evidently constricting and uncongenial; she was unable to put much of contemporary reality or her own personality into her work. Later she was to say, "To hell with easy rhythms—/ sloppy mules that anyone can/ kick off or step into." The statement is unjust, for it is difficult for "anyone" to write well in traditional measures, but it suggests her feeling of release when she discovered the free forms of projective verse.

Many of the poems in *The Double Image* were written during the war years, but, although they succeed in conveying the anxieties of the time, they fail to render the particular sights and sounds of England at war. (Miss Levertov was a nurse in London hospitals at that time.) They lack the vividness that was later to become a feature of her style. She is fairly successful in a poem entitled "Christmas 1944," in which she describes a Christmas tree, a fire in the hearth, and cards from absent friends:

> Though we are safe
> in a flickering circle of winter festival
> we dare not laugh; or if we laugh, we lie,
> hearing hatred crackle in the coal,
> the voice of treason, the voice of love.

And she achieves an image of hopeful love, without fear of change, in a poem entitled "The Past Can Wait":

O, be deaf to what they say—
rumours of distant winters and a broken bough—
now when your love is a candle to dazzle the day.

The book is divided into two parts. The first part is entitled "Fears" and projects the anxieties of growing up, of moving from Eden into a world of time, and experiencing change, death, and loneliness, which the poet sees as inescapable even in times of intense union with others. The poems of the second part, entitled "Promises," are less gloomy and melancholy and less convincing. They seem willed: the poet is determined to find reassurance in the seasonal round, in the upbeat that spring suggests. For example, after describing a wooden, expressionless population which never returns a traveler's "look of love," Miss Levertov finds hope, a stir of life, "in the elusive avenue/ skirting the town" where she hears "the sound of tears/ break on the night as rain into a lake." And she ends the book on this Shelleyan note:

Though once the trouble on a sleeping face
lay like a leopard in the shade of joy,
to-night I know that pain is only a part
of fierce and beautiful life; that silent stone
anticipates the solitudes of Spring
I had no heart for; and I know the hour
grows like a branch, the promise of bright leaves.

Eleven years passed before Miss Levertov published another book, *Here and Now* (1957). Many changes occurred in the interval. She left England, where she was born of Russian and Welsh parents, and came to the United States as the wife of Mitchell Goodman, an American writer whom she had met on a tour of France. Here she became interested in the work of the *Origin* and Black Mountain poets and redirected her poetic career. Her new style was open in form, conversational in rhythm and idiom, and full of brilliant perceptions of reality.

In her pronouncements on poetry Miss Levertov has made clear that, like many of her associates, she believes "poets are instruments on which the power of poetry plays." But she does not subscribe to any mystique of spontaneity, for poets "are also *makers*, craftsmen: It is given to the seer to see, but it is then his responsibility to communicate what he sees, that they who cannot see may see, since we are 'members one of another.'"

Unlike Charles Olson, who believes that form is merely an extension of content, Miss Levertov stresses the importance of form: "I believe content determines form, and yet that content is discovered only *in* form." This paradoxical statement seems to mean that a poet's formal commitments, his way of handling words and lines, assist in the selection and revelation of content. As to the nature of this content, Miss Levertov insists that "a violent imitation of the horrors of our time" is not the concern of poetry. "I long," she says, "for poems of an inner harmony in utter contrast to the chaos in which they exist." This stress on the *stasis* or inner harmony of poetry, the aim of which is vision, is opposed to the *kinesis* of works of persuasion, the aim of which is action.

In *Here and Now*, Miss Levertov tries to achieve the inner poetic harmony she admires by focusing not on the psychological upheavals of the private life or on the disasters of the public life, but on the objects that the world offers so munificently for the poet's examination. She renders these objects with loving exactness and so makes them yield meanings and feelings that radiate into the moral, psychological, and even political realms. Her themes have a wide range. She describes roses in a gypsy's window, looking "as unreal/ as real roses," a bank teller shuffling bank notes, a bird caught overnight in a room, Christmas trees on a bank's façade, hands hovering over piano keys, and the look of the earth when a bucket of water is thrown on it, "suddenly black." As the title of the book indicates, the poems are focused on the present; they are records of actual or probable experience, not evocations of archetypes.

In her third book, *Overland to the Islands* (1958), Miss Levertov keeps on describing the world in vivid, precise, carefully controlled lines. Nothing in the contemporary scene is intractable to her: she describes a car climbing up a hill, dishes settling in a sink, the faces of slum children, a supermarket in Mexico, boys hitting bottles set on a wall. In "Illustrious Ancestors" she says that she would like to make poems "direct as what birds said,/ hard as a floor, sound as a bench,/ mysterious as the silence when the tailor/ would pause with his needle in the air." And she does precisely that in the title poem, "Overland to the Islands," in which she sketches a dog moving across a field:

> Under his feet
> rocks and mud, his imagination, sniffing,
> engaged in its perceptions—dancing
> edgeways, there's nothing
> the dog disdains on his way,
> nevertheless he
> keeps moving, changing
> pace and approach but
> not direction—"every step an arrival."

There is a similar exactness, combined with an air of mystery, in a poem entitled "Sunday Afternoon," in which the daughters of a coffee merchant are shown taking off the white dresses they had worn at their First Communion and running about the neighborhood in the late afternoon, "alive, alive, kicking a basketball, wear-ing/ other new dresses, of bloodred velvet."

Miss Levertov is sometimes amused by people, but she never laughs at them or satirizes them: she is too

humane, too generous in spirit to do that: she takes
everyone very seriously. She sympathizes with all loneliness and sorrows over all deprivation, as she does in the
poem "Something" where she talks about the mobility
of Puerto Rican children: "Their faces change/ from
moment to moment/ both the beautiful ones and those/
deformed by want." In another poem, "Pure Products,"
she describes a couple of American tourists in Mexico
looking for whole-wheat flour, but she does not allow
herself to be malicious. This is how she characterizes
them:

> They are dying
> in their gentleness, adorned
> with wrinkled apple smiles—nothing
> remains for them
> but to live a little, invoking
> the old powers.

The poet's characteristic powers are evident in her
fourth book also, *With Eyes at the Back of Our Heads*
(1960). One senses her confidence in her vision and her
art. And one senses a deepening awareness of the terrors
of life. She sees that a human being can work through
the darkest experiences to a new equilibrium, a reorder-
ing of schedule. This seems to be the meaning of "A
Ring of Changes":

> What holds us upright, once we have faced
> immeasurable darkness, the black point

at our eyes' center? Were we suspended,
museum butterflies, by a filament, from a hidden nail?
Has it broken when we begin to
fall, slowly, without desire?
(But we don't fall. The floor is flat, the round earth
is flat, and we stand on it, and though we lie down
and fill our lungs with choking dust
and spread our arms to make a cross
after a while we rise and creep away,
walk from one room to another
"on our feet again.")

A number of poems in the new book are about the making of poems and other works of art. These are really tributes to the life of the imagination, the power to see "with eyes at the back of our heads." Like Wallace Stevens, Miss Levertov identifies the imagination with God, for she sees it as recreating "what is gone," making poems "out of the whole/ cloth of silence." She says the imagination "swims,/ shining dark-scaled fish,/ swims and waits, flashes, waits and/ wavers, shining of its own light." And it has the power to triumph over time, for while "Our lives flower and pass," poems and works of imagination "live in eternity." Like all poets, Miss Levertov dreams of transcendence.

In her next two books, *The Jacob's Ladder* (1961) and *O Taste and See* (1964), Miss Levertov's powers of exact observation appear undiminished. In some poems they are put at the service of her social concern. She sympathizes with a solitary blind man in the subway and with the waves of immigrants in the New World trying to make their adjustments. She says that, like them, she knows what it means to lose an Old World, to pick up "fragments of the New World slowly,/ not knowing how to put them together nor how to join/ image with image." Her social-ethical concern is especially evident in the long poem entitled "During the Eichmann Trial," in which she characterizes the man who ordered the murder of millions of people in Nazi concentration camps during World War II as a "pitiful man whom none/ pity, whom all/ must pity if they look/ into their own face." Miss Levertov implies that we are all "members/ one of another," in doing evil as in doing good. Like Hannah Arendt, she is aware of "the banality of evil" and its omnipresence, and she insists, as an ethical imperative in every man's life, that the struggle against it must be continuous. She asks every man to look up "from his being" to the being of others. She asks him to create a Jacob's ladder of deeds along which multitudes of angels may descend and ascend.

The popular poetry of the 1950's and 1960's is not the sentimental, rhymed verse of the newpaper poets but the uninhibited, open-form poetry of the "beat generation," which came into prominence in the middle 1950's and had a tremendous vogue for about five years. The howls of the beat generation have been reverberating ever since in the verse of young rebels everywhere. The term "beat generation" seems to have been coined by Jack Kerouac to characterize his friends. It has the resonance of complex connotations. In a religious sense, "beatness" is related to "beatitude" and suggests the

166

innocence, blessedness, and raptness of the hip angel aspiring to be united with the One. In a musical sense, it implies the keeping of a beat, the jazz beat, and so being in harmony with others in the groove, those who can be turned on to the truth. And, in a sociological and psychological sense, it describes the condition of the outsider, the man who is down and out, who looks at "square" society from the peripheries and rejects its disciplines, goals, and values.

The beat poets are certainly disaffiliated. Their rebellion is a sort of non-programmatic leftism or anarchism vastly different from the revolutionary commitments of the youth of the 1930's and equally different from the "new leftism" of the "angry young men" in England, who came into prominence at about the same time. The beat poets are disillusioned not only with middle-class society, with what they regard as its hypocrisy and conformity, but also with the slogans and futile sectarianism of the political radicals. The beat poets favor gratification in the present, living each moment for whatever content of pain or pleasure it may have, pushing experience as far as it will go, and registering only those truths that can be authenticated by personal experience. Authenticity of behavior has meant, for some, a casualness or coolness of reaction to all social pressures. Features of beat life have been unconventional clothing, hairiness, talk about nakedness, experiments with sex and drugs, and parties at which the mood ranges from jazz to blues to "digging the silence."

The public life of the beat poets has consisted of reading appearances in coffeehouses, colleges, and art galleries, chiefly in New York and San Francisco. They obviously enjoy direct contact with live audiences and cater to them with highly repetitive, easily caught lines, sometimes recited to jazz accompaniment. Sometimes the verse is composed on the spot. Because of its irreverence, bawdiness, "sick humor," and freewheeling political satire, this beat poetry has proved to be immensely popular.

And in book form, too, beat poetry has been popular. Allen Ginsberg's *Howl*, which came out in 1956 and was temporarily banned by the San Francisco police because of alleged obscenity, sold over 50,000 copies within a few years. The books of Gregory Corso and Lawrence Ferlinghetti also have had large sales.

A great many poets have been associated with the beat movement, among them Jack Kerouac (who is better as a novelist), Ted Joans, Peter Orlovsky, and Ray Bremser, but the three principal figures are Allen Ginsberg, Lawrence Ferlinghetti, and Gregory Corso. Ferlinghetti is the author of the following collections of verse: *Pictures of the Gone World* (1955), *A Coney Island of the Mind* (1958), and *Tentative Description of a Dinner Given to Promote the Impeachment of Presi-*

dent Eisenhower (1958). He has also published a novel, *Her* (1960). Gregory Corso is the author of these books of verse: *The Vestal Lady on Brattle* (1955), *Gasoline* (1958), *Bomb* (1959), *The Happy Birthday of Death* (1960), and *Long Live Man* (1962). He has also written a novel, *The American Express* (1961).

All of these poets take their rhythmic beat from Charles Olson and the other practitioners of projective verse. Like them, they talk about the breath-conditioned line, the importance of making perception follow perception, and the value of free, organic, spontaneous expression.

Allen Ginsberg, of course, is the most important of the beat poets. His first book, *Howl and Other Poems*, expresses some of the themes and attitudes of the whole group: their aspiration toward holiness and blessedness, their attacks on the establishment from a generally leftist but unprogrammatic point of view, and their sense of the interrelationship between madness, sex, drug addiction, and poverty. The title poem, in fact, purports to speak for a whole generation; Ginsberg commiserates with what he calls the "best minds of my generation," whom he describes in the first part as "destroyed by madness." He shows them "yearning for the ancient heavenly connection to the starry dynamo in the machinery of night" but behaving irrationally, subject to hallucinations. He shows them taking drugs, distributing "Supercommunist pamphlets in Union Square," enjoying sex with "saintly motorcyclists," and exhibiting themselves on rooftops until they "are dragged off the roof waving genitals and manuscripts." In the second part of the poem Ginsberg ascribes the madness of his generation to the baleful influence of Moloch, the god of power, who "bashed open their skulls and ate up their brains and imagination." In the third part the poet concentrates on the destiny of one man, Carl Solomon, who has gone mad and is shut up in a mental hospital where he is pacified with electric shocks. The poet identifies with him, sympathizes with his suffering, and projects an imaginary moment of freedom for both, when the soul's airplanes "drop angelic bombs" over the world and all walls collapse and the poet can shout to his friend: "O victory forget your underwear we're free."

"Howl" is a grimly serious poem, but it has flights of humor, and this mingling of the solemn and the comic is characteristic of other poems in the collection as well. There is, for example, "A Supermarket in California," in which the poet experiences a headache as he enters a supermarket and then happily encounters Walt Whitman "poking among the meats in the refrigerator and eyeing the grocery boys." There is the poem "America," in which Ginsberg takes the country to task for failing to be angelic, for failing to realize its promise; he asks with mock naïveté, "When will you be worthy of your million Trotskyites?" And he ends the poem with the wild line, "America I'm putting my queer shoulder to the wheel."

Ginsberg's idealism, muted though it sometimes seems, pervades the whole book. In "Sunflower Sutra," for example, he describes a dusty, dying sunflower by a railroad track and rejects the appearance as unreal: "We're not our skins of grime, we're not our dread bleak dusty imageless locomotive, we're all beautiful golden sunflowers inside." And he ends his book with a poem entitled "In Back of the Real," in which a "tough spikey ugly flower" is said to suggest "the form of the great yellow/ Rose" which is "the flower of the World." Ginsberg keeps climbing toward realms of spirit.

His second book, *Kaddish and Other Poems: 1958–1960*, appeared in 1961. "Kaddish," the title poem, is a lament for his mother, who died in a mental hospital of a stroke after a bitter life of poverty and turmoil as a Russian immigrant in Newark. It is essentially Ginsberg's anguished remembrance of his mother's suffering, so anguished that when he first read the poem in its entirety to a *Catholic Worker* audience on Chrystie Street in New York, he broke into tears. The first two parts of the poem provide details of Naomi's girlhood and marriage to Louis Ginsberg, the poet; her Communist affiliations; and her developing paranoia, which took the form of a fear of Hitler and spies and led to her confinement in various rest homes and hospitals, where she endured shock treatments and gradually withdrew from the world, failing to recognize members of her own family, even Allen himself on his last visit to her, thinking him a spy. She begged him not to murder her: "I'm not a bad girl," she said. After her death the poet received a letter from her, mailed before her death, which provides a moment of illumination in the poem: "The key is in the window, the key is in the sunlight at the window—I have the key—Get married Allen don't take drugs—the key is in the bars, in the sunlight in the window." This revelation is followed by a hymn of acceptance addressed to God, a passage in which the significance of the phrase "the key is in the sunlight" is meditated, and two pages devoted to an evocation of the image of Naomi, focusing on her eyes. The poem concludes with images of crows hovering over the gravestones in the Long Island cemetery where Ginsberg's mother is buried. They suggest the crows over the wheat field in one of van Gogh's last paintings.

A feature of Ginsberg's second collection of poems is an emphasis on vision-producing drugs. There is a poem entitled "Laughing Gas" and another entitled "Mescaline." Three other poems, according to a note in the book, "record visions experienced after drinking ayahuasca, an Amazon spiritual potion. The message is: Widen the area of consciousness." In all of these poems the poet yearns for mystic illumination, for truths beyond the register of the senses. In "Magic

Psalm," for example, he wishes to rise beyond desire to the "calm water of the universe." In the following poem, "The Reply," God is said to answer with doom: the poet is "annulled." The tone is fearful; the poet is humble; and the universe "turns inside out to devour" him. But in the third poem, "The End," he sees himself as part of an endless process of creation; he returns from death again and again, thrilled with his "deathlessness." It is the familiar cycle of birth, death, and rebirth, and one hardly needs ayahuasca to be reminded of it.

In 1961, Ginsberg also published *Empty Mirror: Early Poems,* which contained previously uncollected verse. One of the poems, "In Society," records an amusing dream of 1947 in which the poet finds himself at a party where a "fluffy female" glares at him and declares, "I don't like you." Stung, the poet cries out, "Why you narcissistic bitch!" He launches into a tirade, "inspired at/ last, dominating the whole room." Another interesting poem is "The Bricklayer's Lunch Hour," in which Ginsberg describes tenderly, carefully, a young bricklayer eating his lunch and playing with a kitten that comes along.

Ginsberg's fourth book, *Reality Sandwiches,* appeared in 1963. It is characterized by restlessness, as many of the poems are little more than diary records of trips to Havana, Seattle, Peru, Mexico, San Francisco, and elsewhere. Like other members of the beat generation, Ginsberg is forever on the road in search of illumination. The best poem in the book is one entitled "Love Poem on Theme by Whitman," in which the poet slides into bed between a bride and a bridegroom and enjoys their love-making, rising "replenished with last intimate gestures and kisses of farewell."

In assessing the work of Allen Ginsberg, one can say that he is a sort of Theodore Dreiser of American poetry. He is as awkward in phrase and as ungainly in manner as that novelist often was. His poems find their shape only after fighting almost insuperable obstacles in rhythm, grammar, and diction. Sometimes his phrase-making is completely ludicrous. Although it is true that incongruities can produce humor and counteract senti-mentality, the poet must keep them under control in order to prevent them from destroying the mood he is trying to create. For example, in describing the death of his mother, Ginsberg says: "Magnificent, mourned no more, marred of heart, mind behind, married dreamed, mortal changed—Ass and face done with murder." The reader is not shocked by this inept reference to "Ass and face"; he is merely annoyed by the mood-destroying inappropriateness of the phrase in a passage intended to suggest solemnity and sorrow.

And yet, for all his crudity, Ginsberg does convey a sense of the holiness of all things, the ugly and the beautiful alike. He keeps building bridges between them for the passage of love.

In the late 1950's three Minnesota poets—Robert Bly, James Wright, and William Duffy—joined two New York poets—Robert Kelly and Jerome Rothenberg—in launching a movement toward subjectivism in American poetry. They rejected the objective image of the Imagists of 1910 and championed the subjective image or the image freighted with unconscious elements, in the fashion of the Surrealists. Although they denied any influence from the Charles Olson-inspired groups (Robert Bly insists that his work would have existed in its present character even if Olson had never written), they were in general agreement with them that traditional metrics of the accent-counting variety were unsatisfactory in suggesting American space, time, and experience; they concurred in the opinion that new organizations of sound, in free forms, were essential for the continuing vitality of American poetry. But they disliked what they regarded as the bareness of much American verse and complained about the diffuse, prosaic quality of most of the work of their contemporaries. They were determined to avoid these defects in their own verse by concentrating on the image, for they felt that a poem lived in its imagery. And they began a campaign against abstraction by urging other poets to read the masters of modern French and Spanish poetry, those who had written wildly and had looked inward without fear or shame, poets like Rimbaud and Lorca. Robert Bly and William Duffy issued a magazine, *The Fifties* (renamed *The Sixties* as the new decade began), in which they published free-form verse full of imagery and in which they fought a battle against abstract statement and easy, conscience-lulling metrics. The New York group published a magazine called *Trobar*, in the pages of which Robert Kelly fought a similar battle in behalf of the "deep image" in poetry. His article, "Notes on the Poetry of the Deep Image," which appeared in *Trobar 2* (1961), pp. 14–15, is an important document of the movement and bears the same relationship to deep-image poetry that Charles Olson's article on projective verse, in *Poetry New York*, bears to the movement that produced Denise Levertov, Robert Creeley, and Robert Duncan.

In his article Kelly acknowledges his indebtedness to Jerome Rothenberg for the phrase "deep image." The term refers to a concrete particular that has attracted and operates in a context of powerful feelings and associations in the unconscious of the poet and evokes a similar context in the unconscious of the reader when it appears in an imaginatively conceived and ordered poem. The deep image carries its original affective power in a pattern of new and even surprising verbal combinations, contributing to their force. As Kelly puts it, "Poetry, like dream reality, is the juncture of the experienced with the never-experienced. Like waking reality, it is the fulfilment of the imagined and the unimagined."

Kelly has great respect for projective verse, which he says "offers a method of resolving breath and line" and "allows tremendous stress on the last verbal unit in the line, a stress exploited not for key words but for key silences, stretching out to vital and peripheral words." But his concern is to "substitute the centrality of image for the centrality of syllable and line as a way of access to the happening of a poem." He goes on to say that "When the image, prima materia, is lacking, the verbal gesture is quickly emptied: the poem elapses instead of happening. The fundamental rhythm of the poem is the rhythm of the images; their textures, their contents, offer supplementary rhythms."

On the important matters of the ordering of images and their relationship to each other, Kelly has this to say: "Basically, the fullest force is possible only by means of the successful employment of one image's position in a context of other images; the image, after its first appearance as dark sound, still lingers as a resonance. This resonance must be controlled, and the effective means of control are the acoustics of the space intervening between one image and the next. The subsequent image is conditioned, made to work, by the image that precedes it, and conditions, as it is finally conditioned by, the image that follows it: through the whole poem. The first image to appear in an André Breton poem will normally dominate all subsequent images and the poem as a whole, even when the reader seems to have forgotten it."

Like most contemporary poets, Kelly takes the position that only the language of living people is an appropriate basis for poetry and that it must come across without obstructions, without "cuteness or distraction." But this is not to say that the poet is limited to the clichés of everyday speech; Kelly says that newness is possible because "images mold their own expressions." And he insists that the "language of the image" must be urgent: "The need for urgency, for tension in the work itself, cannot be exaggerated. The language of deep images restores the poetry of desperation."

Kelly's sense of the importance of the deep image is shared by Robert Bly, who feels that an inward look can vitalize any poet's work. In "Some Thoughts on Lorca and René Char," an article published in *The Fifties*, Third Issue (1959), pp. 7–9, Bly contrasts French poetry of the nineteenth century with American poetry of the 1930's and 1940's and finds the latter deficient in magic: "Beginning with Baudelaire, French poetry went through a dark valley, a valley filled with black pools, lions, jungles, turbid rivers, dead men hanging from trees, wolves eating the feathers of birds, thunder hanging over doors, images of seas, sailors, drunken boats, maggots eating a corpse with the sound of a sower sowing grain, endless voyages, vast bleak skies, huge birds, continual rain. This immersion has given French poetry its strength, its rich soil, whereas our soil is thin and rocky, and the poetry of the 30's and 40's increasingly resembles a flower cut off above the ground, slowly withering." He is dissatisfied with the work of Pound and Eliot because, in his opinion, neither poet is willing to face the unconscious: their Puritanism prevents it. He goes on to say that "Even the Imagists were misnamed: they did not write in images from the unconscious, as Lorca or Neruda, but in simple pictures, such as 'petals on a wet black bough,' and Pound, for instance, continues to write in pictures, writing as great a poetry as is possible, which in his case is very great, using nothing but pictures, but still, pictures are not images. And without these true images, this water from the unconscious, the language continues to dry up."

The emphasis that Bly, Kelly, and their associates have put on the deep image has had the salutary effect of providing a partial corrective to the projective-verse movement, with its commitment to field composition and the equivalence of line and breath to the exclusion of a great many other matters. One certainly cannot quarrel with the notion that poetry should have imagery, whether of the deep or surface variety. But the poets of the subjective-image movement tend to neglect another important element of poetry, and that is, simply, action or plot. In a great deal of classic poetry an incident occurs to engage the opposites of which the poem is made; this incident makes for drama, tension, force, and suggests the world as we know it. The neglect of drama makes for static, quiet, meditative verse. In unskillful hands, this verse consists of coagulations of images that do not sort out. Fortunately this does not happen in the work of James Wright and Robert Bly.

(a)   James Wright

James Wright has produced some of the best poems of the new subjectivism.

He did not, however, begin as a poet of subjective images. His first book, *The Green Wall* (1957), is largely traditional, and in iambic measure, which he handles with considerable skill. Only occasionally does one feel a discordance between the subject matter and the metrical and stanzaic frames in which the poet chooses to cast it. For example, "A Poem About George Doty in the Death House" deals with the last days of a rapist in a leaping trimeter that seems a little inappropriate:

> Close to the wall inside,
> Immured, empty of love,
> A man I have wondered of
> Lies patient, vacant-eyed.
> A month and a day ago
> He stopped his car and found
> A girl on the darkening ground
> And killed her in the snow.

Of course it is true that many fine folk ballads tell gruesome stories in rollicking rhythms, and sometimes brilliantly ironic effects can be achieved by contrasting the theme and the meter of a poem, but here the effect is insensitive, especially as the poet claims, at the end of the poem, that he mourns for the rapist's soul but not for "the homely girl whose cry/ Crumbled his pleading kiss."

But this withdrawal of empathy from the girl seems

like an unfortunate rhetorical device, a means of achieving emphasis, for the book as a whole reveals the poet's all-encompassing sympathy, his almost Oriental assumption of all the roles of life. He has a few poems about landscapes, about the seasonal ebb and flow, but for the most part he writes about people, about simple, desperate, unhappy people like those who populate the poems of Edwin Arlington Robinson and Robert Frost. He describes a deaf child, a family doctor, a prostitute, a Lesbian, and a fugitive from the law. Sickness and death figure prominently; one of the poems, about a dead dog, is reminiscent of Richard Eberhart's famous poem about a decaying groundhog. Wright makes note of the facts of life, but not dispassionately; he is always profoundly involved.

In his second book, *Saint Judas* (1959), Wright is looser in his metrics; the technique is still traditional, but there is an ease of manner that recalls Frost.

The subject matter is still largely "dark." For instance, there are several poems about death. There are poems about a drunken old man, a man drowning, a child floating in oil slick while its mother curses the sea "Washing its hands." There are also poems about the execution of Caryl Chessman and a visit to the grave of another executed murderer. The book ends with a striking poem about Judas, who, on an errand to kill himself, sees a man being beaten by a gang of hoodlums.

His love goes out to him: "Flayed without hope,/ I held the man for nothing in my arms."

Wright's third book, *The Branch Will Not Break* (1963), represents a drastic change in technique, subject matter, and tone. First of all, it is evident that in the course of the three years preceding the publication of the new book Wright had abandoned the accentual-syllabic metrics of tradition for the free forms initiated by the followers of Charles Olson. In the second place, it is clear that he has now committed himself to the psychological resonance of deep imagery. And, in the third place, he has widened his scope by including subject matter that is not unrelievedly gloomy. He is still aware of the darkness around him, but he often ends his poems on an upbeat. Consider, for example, "A Dream of Burial," with which the book ends:

> Nothing was left of me
> But my right foot
> And my left shoulder.
> They lay white as a skein of a spider floating
> In a field of snow toward a dark building
> Tilted and stained by wind.
> Inside the dream, I dreamed on.
>
> A parade of old women
> Sang softly above me,
> Faint mosquitoes near still water.

So I waited, in my corridor.
I listened for the sea
To call me.
I knew that, somewhere outside, the horse
Stood saddled, browsing in grass,
Waiting for me.

The poem is obviously in free form; it has an imagery of complex associations; and it ends on an upbeat: the waiting horse points to a resurrection for the dead man's bones.

Another sign of the new tone is the very title of the book. It comes from a passage in which the poet looks at a jay "springing up and down,/ On a branch." He remarks that the jay "knows as well as I do/ That the branch will not break." This is an astonishing assertion; it represents a measure of confidence in the reality and continuity of the world that was wholly absent from the first two books. Or consider the poem entitled "A Blessing," in which the poet describes an Indian pony that once came up to him and "nuzzled" his "left hand." He is tremendously moved by the experience: "Suddenly I realize/ That if I stepped out of my body I would break/ Into blossom."

But it must be admitted that Wright does not always succeed in his new poems. His "deep image" does not always reverberate according to plan because the occasion, the situation described in the poem, is too slight for the emotion that the poet says he is feeling: the details do not add up to the indicated experience. For example, in "Lying in a Hammock at William Duffy's Farm in Pine Island, Minnesota," Wright offers a number of rather pleasant descriptive details of an afternoon and evening and then concludes, without any sort of preparation: "I have wasted my life." This sort of observation, coming at the end of a poem, can have a tremendous impact if it represents a reversal of an established direction, but in this poem there is no real contrast and the line fails.

Nevertheless, James Wright is a poet from whom one can expect miracles.

(b)   Robert Bly

Robert Bly has published one book, *Silence in the Snowy Fields* (1962). He is a poet of Western space, solitude, and silence. He writes poems about driving a car through Ohio, hunting pheasants, watering a horse, getting up early in the morning, and watching Minnesota cornfields, lakes, and woods under the siege of rain, snow, and sun. His distinction in treating these subjects lies in the freshness of his "deep images," which invest the scene he describes with an intense subjectivity and a feeling of the irremediable loneliness of man, who can never make contact with the things of the world. Bly speaks of "the loneliness hiding in grass and weeds/ That lies near a man over thirty, and suddenly enters."

This subjectivity is also evident in such lines as these: "Inside me there is a confusion of swallows,/ Birds flying through the smoke,/ And horses galloping excitedly on fields of short grass." And in a haiku-like poem entitled "Watering the Horse" one finds both subjectivity and a sense of the pathos of all human activity:

How strange to think of giving up all ambition!
Suddenly I see with such clear eyes
The white flake of snow
That has just fallen in the horse's mane!

Another characteristic poem is "Snowfall in the Afternoon," which has simple imagery that stirs complex emotions related to such opposites as light and darkness, contentment and insecurity, vision and blindness:

I

The grass is half-covered with snow.
It was the sort of snowfall that starts in late afternoon,
And now the little houses of the grass are growing dark.

II

If I reached my hands down, near the earth,
I could take handfuls of darkness!
A darkness was always there, which we never noticed.

III

As the snow grows heavier, the cornstalks fade farther
    away,
And the barn moves nearer to the house.
The barn moves all alone in the growing storm.

IV

The barn is full of corn, and moving toward us now,
Like a hulk blown toward us in a storm at sea;
All the sailors on deck have been blind for many years.

It is evident that Robert Bly's theory and practice
cohere. His poetic voice is clear, quiet, and appealing,
and it has the resonance that only powerful pressures at
great depths can provide.

(a) John Ashbery

John Ashbery is one of the most original of contemporary poets. His four books of poems, *Turandot and Other Poems* (1953), *Some Trees* (1956), *The Poems* (1960), and *The Tennis Court Oath* (1962) are full of startling metaphors and fresh juxtapositions of words and perceptions. He keeps pushing the limits of language; he lives on the most thinly held, the most dangerous, frontiers. His impatience with the merely remembered phrase is evident in every line, though he occasionally uses a cliché to evoke a standard response which he then swamps with irony. He is not without antecedents and influences, however. He has gone to school to Wallace Stevens, from whom he gets both elegance and a furious concentration; to the French Surrealist poets, who have taught him to find fresh images in immersions in the subconscious; and to the "action" painters of the New York School of the 1950's, who have taught him to work with abandon at his canvas and to pray for happy accidents. But his voice is unmistakably his own; it is a voice that does not falter in a world of discontinuities. As a matter of fact, he seems to fear too much coherence as being a form of dishonesty or falseness. An orderly syntax sometimes forces the poet to lie, to say easy things that he had not intended, that are not of his own experience.

Ashbery's weakness is a curious opaqueness, at times, that comes from tenuousness or paucity of subject matter. But he comments—tangentially—on many familiar themes: love (seen as a form of touching, like intertwined trees), time ("we have not avoided our destiny/ By weeding out the old people"), art, America, Europe, the desperation of the man on the road, and the unbearable boredom of industrial society from which one can be saved only by daydreaming. In the poem "The Instruction Manual," the speaker imagines vivid flirtations in a public square in Guadalajara as a form of escape from the task of writing an instruction manual on the uses of a new metal.

Technically, Ashbery is in debt to projective verse, for he works in free forms even when he invokes the

"spirit" of the sonnet, canzone, or pantoum. Here is a
sample of his work, a poem entitled "A White Paper":

> And if he thought that
> All was foreign—
> As, gas and petrol, en-
> gine full of seeds, barking to hear the night
> The political contaminations
>
> Of what he spoke,
> Spotted azaleas brought to meet him
> Sitting next day
> The judge, emotions,
> The crushed paper heaps.

The images of this brilliant poem suggest an American
tourist's reaction to foreign places: the whirl of sensory
impressions, the judgments he makes, the distress he
feels at not touching, etc. The poem is entitled "A
White Paper" because the tourist's predicament is always an international crisis of sorts, to him, requiring
a document in explanation and justification.

(b)   James Dickey

James Dickey has published three books of poems in
rapid succession: *Into the Stone,* part of vol. 7 of *Poets*

of Today (1960), *Drowning with Others* (1962), and
Helmets (1964). His subject matter comes largely from
three areas of experience: country life, with its images
of plants and animals and such activities as hunting and
swimming; the Second World War, in which the poet
participated in the Pacific war theater and learned how
men behave in extreme situations; and family relations
—incidents and feelings by means of which the poet
examines his ties with his parents, on the one hand,
and with his children, on the other, achieving ranges
of understanding across and beyond time. Dickey
handles this subject matter with great resourcefulness.
He pursues an incident or a set of relations doggedly
until he wrings every drop of meaning from it; he enjoys working up an almost metaphysical intricacy of
metaphor, carrying it through until all the tensions of a
poem are resolved. In this way he produces *finished*
poems, and so it is not surprising that he is immensely
popular with readers who fear discontinuity. Moreover,
his values are sound, trustworthy; there is no nonsense
or wildness in his point of view; he isn't likely to startle
the reader by sticking out his tongue at him. For example, he sympathizes with the fox that is being pur-
sued by hounds; he understands the guilt and sorrow of
a lifeguard who fails to save a drowning boy; he recognizes the humanity of the Japanese enemy; and he is
moved by the plight of derelicts in the Bowery. It is only

in his love poems that there is a movement outside the boundaries of approved emotion, as in "Cherrylog Road," a poem in which a young man has a sex experience with his girl in the back seat of an old car in a junk yard. But here the reader is obviously expected to smile and brood a little about the urgency of sexual desire in youth.

Dickey's technique is a compromise between traditional forms and the free forms of the 1960's. He works in stanzaic units of four, five, and six lines and sometimes uses rhyme to point up his meaning. But his line is rhythmically free, at times approximating an accentual measure of three, four, or five beats. The verse moves in an orderly syntax without much surprise or wildness of phrase. The quality of Dickey's work can be suggested by "The Lifeguard," in which a lifeguard who has failed to save a drowning boy returns to the scene of his failure at night and suffers the remorse of the savior who fails to save. He imagines he sees the boy again. The poem ends with this stanza:

> I wash the black mud from my hands.
> On a light given off by the grave
> I kneel in the quick of the moon
> At the heart of a distant forest
> And hold in my arms a child
> Of water, water, water.

Clearly, this is moving, sincere, unpretentious writing.

(c)   *Alan Dugan*

Alan Dugan's irreverent wit ranges across the whole social scene for targets; in *Poems* (1961) and *Poems 2* (1963) he attacks the conformity and soul-stifling discipline of Army life and the business routines of civilian life, which demand that a person do "accounts receivable as fast/ as steel machines and out-/ talk telephones." He is especially bitter about unemployment, about cooling one's heels in an outer office while a job interviewer consults his convenience. He seems more than a little fearful of life in general, for he speaks of getting up in the morning and walking out into the "daily accident." He distrusts all slogans, all prophecy, and questions all received values, the precepts of inherited morality, which he sees as a "bad joke like everything else." Human beings are, to him, "prisoners of this world"; they are imprisoned in their skins, their jobs, their communities, the world they never made. His sardonic view of humanity does not spare himself or his family. In "Fabrication of Ancestors" he describes Old Billy Blue Balls, "shot in the ass in the Civil War." In "Elegy," which is about his father's funeral, he describes not the grief of the family but Uncle Robert taking a drink while shaving and leaving "soap-suds in the whiskey."

It is a pleasure to read Dugan because of the very fact that nothing is sacred to him. Seeing everything in an unconventional way, he can startle the reader into a fresh perception of ordinary realities. His idiom is strictly contemporary, strictly American, and his wittiest effects are produced by the incongruity between his colloquial diction and his subjects, which are often as serious as the French war in Algeria or unemployment or the Irish censorship. He is not always smooth or competent as a craftsman, but he is honest in his treatment of what he sees. His verse form is largely free, though he sometimes works in a four-foot or five-foot metrical pattern. At his worst he lacks intensity and verges on light verse; at his best he produces a witty, serious poem like "Life Comparison":

> Picked up, a hermit crab who seems
> to curl up in a dead snail's shell
> from cowardice, attacks the thumb
> sustaining him in extraordinary air,
> regardless, and if he is attacked
> by borers or the other enemies of shells,
> he crawls out, raw at the rear!,
> to find a new place, thus exposed.
> So, he does what is appropriate
> within his means, within a case,
> and fails: oh he could not bite off

the top whorl of my fingerprint,
although he tried. Therefore, I put
him back to sea for courage, for
his doing what he thinks he has to do
while shrinking, and to propitiate
my own incommensurate enemies,
the firms, establishment, and state.

(d) LeRoi Jones

Two observations can be made about American Negro
poets of the recent past. The first is that they are becoming increasingly deft and sophisticated in the handling of prevailing poetic styles. Evidence for this observation can be found in the work of such poets as
Melvin B. Tolson, Owen Dodson, Margaret Walker,
Gwendolyn Brooks, and Gloria Oden. The second is
that they are moving toward a new social consciousness
associated with "negritude," a renewed emphasis on the
value of the black man and a new militancy in winning
social, economic, educational, and sexual equality for
him. The Negro poets are less and less interested in
"pleasing" a white audience and more and more in-
sistent on telling the truth, whether it pleases or not.
They sometimes insult the white reader in order to
shock him out of his preconceptions about race relations, and they do not spare the feelings of the white

liberal who congratulates himself on the presence of a Negro or two at a party he gives. Among the poets of the more daring, militant awareness are Charles Patterson, Calvin Hernton, and Rolland Snellings, all of them associated with Umbra, a group of Negro poets in New York City.

One of the most talented of the Negro poets is LeRoi Jones, who has both skill as a maker of images and rhythms and daring as an exponent of new sexual and racial subject matter. But this is not to say that Jones is an "engaged" poet; he is too much the cool hipster to trust slogans and programs of any sort, though his sympathy seems generally liberal. He writes about color as an Existential reality, about New York street scenes, about his wife Hettie "in her fifth month," imaginary escapes to fantastic forests, and his alienation from the people of Africa—America being too much a part of him: "My own/ dead souls, my, so called/ people. Africa/ is a foreign place. You are/ as any other sad man here/ american." His technique derives from projective verse; he stresses speech rhythm; and his diction is that of the hipster. In putting his poems together, he is not afraid of discontinuities—they represent reality to him—or prosaic statement if it serves his purpose; but he has more imagery than most hip poets, and he enjoys projecting a wild, comic, sexual fantasy to contrast with the boredom of urban

life, of days confined by steel and concrete. Characteristic of his work is a poem entitled "For Hettie":

> My wife is left-handed.
> Which implies a fierce de-
> termination. A complete other
> worldliness. ITS WEIRD, BABY.
> The way some folks
> are always trying to be
> different. A sin & a shame.
>
> But then, she's been a bohemian
> all of her life . . . black stockings
> refusing to take orders. I sit
> patiently, trying to tell her
> whats right. TAKE THAT DAMM
> PENCIL OUTTA THAT HAND. YOU'RE
> RITING BACKWARDS. & such. But
> to no avail. & it shows
> in her work. Left-handed coffee,
> Left-handed eggs; when she comes
> in at night . . . it's her left hand
> offerd for me to kiss. Damm.
> & now her belly droops over the seat.
> They say it's a child. But
> I ain't quite so sure.

In addition to writing poems, some of which were
collected in *Preface to a Twenty Volume Suicide Note*
(1961) and *The Dead Lecturer* (1964), Jones has been

editing a hospitable, freewheeling verse magazine called *Yugen,* which has been coming out irregularly since 1955. He is the author of a book about the blues, *The Blues People* (1963), and editor of an anthology entitled *The Moderns* (1963). His one-act play, *Dutchman* (1964), was produced at the Cherry Lane Theater in Greenwich Village, and his two short plays, *The Toilet* and *The Slave* (1964), were performed at St. Mark's Playhouse on Second Avenue in New York.

(e)   Louis Simpson

Louis Simpson is the author of *The Arrivistes* (1949), *Good News of Death* (1955), *A Dream of Governors* (1959), and *At the End of the Open Road* (1963). A poet of liberal persuasion, he is interested in public issues, in social and philosophical questions relating to the destiny of Europe and America. He has several poems about the horrors of World War II—one of them is a long narrative poem about the siege of Bastogne; another is about the Nazi butchery in Central Europe. In one of his best poems, "A Dream of Governors," he expresses the chilling thought that the rulers of the world are mad and "bring evil on the land" in order that they "may have a task." In his most recent book, *At the End of the Open Road,* he examines critically the American dream of ever-Westward expansion, symbolized in the open road of Walt Whitman, with its boundless potentialities. Standing on the shore of the Pacific, in California, the poet sees the "same old city-planner, death," even as "The great cloud-wagons move/ Outward still, dreaming of a Pacific." He declares that "Whitman was wrong about the People,/ But right about himself. The land is within./ At the end of the open road we come to ourselves." This is a new realism that Simpson is preaching. He asks us to forget the Adamic innocence of the American past and recognize the seriousness of life in the present; we must cultivate our gardens in full awareness of the imminence of death.

Although he wrote some free verse as a young man, Simpson was deeply committed to traditional technique until 1959; he counted his accented and unaccented syllables carefully and built structures of pleasing but conventional sound, nailed with rhyme. After 1959, largely under the influence of the subjective-image poets, he changed his style drastically. The prosaism of his early work—which required metrics and rhyme in order to give it character as verse—now gave way to rich, fresh, haunting imagery. His philosophical and political speculations achieved a distinction and brilliance that they had lacked before. One can get a sense of Simpson's new direction from a poem entitled "A Farm in Minnesota":

The corn rows walk the earth,
crowding like mankind between the fences,
feeding on sun and rain;
are broken down by hail,
or perish of incalculable drought.

And we who tend them
from the ground up—lieutenants
of this foot cavalry, leaning on fences
to watch our green men never move an inch—
who cares for us?

Our beds are sold at auction.
The Bible, and a sword—these are bequeathed
to children who prefer a modern house.
Our flesh has been consumed
only to make more lives.

But when our heads are planted
under the church, from those empty pods
we rise in the fields of death,
and are gathered by angels,
and shine in the hands of God.

The basic metaphor of this poem—that God is a farmer
—is carefully worked out, but the ending is a little too
predictable from the tenth line, "who cares for us?,"
and induces a conventional response. However, the
poem has a freedom of movement and vividness of
phrase that augur well for Simpson's future as a poet.

(f) William Stafford

William Stafford has published two books of poems, *West of Your City* (1960) and *Traveling Through the Dark* (1962). He is a poet of Existential loneliness and Western space. He seems to write out of an autobiographical impulse, a need to describe and understand his personal experience of the mountains and forests of the Far West. He was born in Kansas, was educated in Iowa, and teaches in Oregon. His memories range widely over these territories and fill his books with images of tornadoes, prairie towns, deserts, mountain-climbing, etc. The technique is not dazzling—there are no verbal fireworks—but Stafford describes the objects of his world carefully and exactly: he has the power to see, the patience to wait for his insights, and the ability to construct strong structures of sound and meaning. He is a sort of Western Robert Frost, forever amazed by the spaces of America, inner and outer. Consider this chilling vision of space and desolation:

> But that state so north it curled behind
> the map in hands of snow and wind,
> clutching the end of no place—
> I hold that state before my face,
> and learn my life.

Sometimes he sees ironic reversals in the old struggle between man and nature and makes wry comment:

> Many go home having "conquered a mountain"—
> they leave their names at the top in a jar
> for snow to remember.

Out of such awareness comes not defeatism but a sharp appraisal of one's surroundings and a self-reliance in tune with nature—reminiscent of Emerson:

> The earth says where you live wear the kind
> of color that your life is (gray shirt for me)
> and by listening with the same bowed head that sings
> draw all into one song, join
> the sparrow on the lawn, and row that easy
> way, the rage without met by the wings
> within that guide you anywhere the wind blows.

(g) May Swenson

May Swenson is the author of *Another Animal*, part of vol. 1 of *Poets of Today* (1954), *A Cage of Spines* (1958), and *To Mix with Time: New and Selected Poems* (1963). Her distinction is that she is able to make poems of ordinary public realities, offering precise images of urban life with an amazed reporter's skill—a reporter with pity—making her reader see clearly what he has merely looked at before. The public squares, parks, subways, museums, and zoos of New York City provide the scenes and incidents for her scrutiny, though there are easy references to Rome, Venice, Paris, and Arles as well, for Miss Swenson has been traveling. She is at her strongest in poems about people riding a subway to work or driving along a highway or feeding pigeons or sitting in a park—lonely people in a world without anchor in the cosmic sea. Characteristic of her work is "Water Picture":

In the pond in the park
all things are doubled:
Long buildings hang and
wriggle gently. Chimneys
are bent legs bouncing
on clouds below. A flag
wags like a fishhook
down there in the sky.

The arched stone bridge
is an eye, with underlid
in the water. In its lens
dip crinkled heads with hats
that don't fall off. Dogs go by,
barking on their backs.
A baby, taken to feed the
ducks, dangles upside-down,
a pink balloon for a buoy.

Treetops deploy a haze of
cherry blooms for roots,
where birds coast belly-up
in the glass bowl of a hill;
from its bottom a bunch
of peanut-munching children
is suspended by their
sneakers, waveringly.

A swan, with twin necks
forming the figure three,
steers between two dimpled
towers doubled. Fondly
hissing, she kisses herself,
and all the scene is troubled:
water-windows splinter,
tree-limbs tangle, the bridge
folds like a fan.

Miss Swenson works in a free verse that is supple
but rather prosaic, despite her picturemaking efforts.
She lacks formal subtlety and profundity of insight.
And some of her poems are badly in need of pruning.
But at her best she succeeds in giving the reader a sense
of what it feels like to be alive in a large American city
in the middle of the twentieth century.

[13] *OBSERVATIONS*

It is clear from this survey of American poetry since 1945—the work of poets who were born in 1910 or later and who came into prominence after the Second World War—that vitality, truthtelling, and technical brilliance are still characteristic of the art. The recent poets have had to work in the shadow of such twentieth-century giants as T. S. Eliot, Robert Frost, Ezra Pound, William Carlos Williams, Marianne Moore, E. E. Cummings, and Hart Crane, but they have not withered in that shadow: they have managed a vigorous new growth that has expanded the subject matter and technical

205

range of American poetry, making it sensitive to every datum of reality, inner and outer.

This triumph was not an easy one; it came about under the pressure of many urgencies and dissatisfactions, tensions, struggles of opposites in the Republic of Poetry. These struggles were manifest in the five trends or movements that characterized American poetry of the 1940's, 1950's, and 1960's. As this survey has already made clear, the careers of the twenty-one poets under study have reflected these trends. There was, first of all, and predictably, a period of involvement in World War II, with its shocking brutalities and disruptions of personal and community life. Characteristic of this period of engagement were such books as Robert Lowell's *Lord Weary's Castle*, with its passionate, brooding concern for the destiny of America; Karl Shapiro's *V-Letter and Other Poems*; and Randall Jarrell's *Little Friend, Little Friend*. After the war there was a disengagement from the horrors of war experience and an attempt at readjustment to civilian patterns of advancement, merrymaking, and boredom, a recovery of lost emotional positions. There was also a gradual withdrawal from politics and social idealism—largely as a result of Cold War disturbances and the hot war in Korea. The poets became increasingly interested in dreams, explorations of psychological states, literary archetypes, and myths with universal reverberations. Characteristic of this trend, which was dominant in the early 1950's, were such books as *A Mask for Janus*, by W. S. Merwin; *The Seven-League Crutches*, by Randall Jarrell; and *Ceremony*, by Richard Wilbur.

The established poets of the 1950's, those who appeared frequently in the literary quarterlies and wrote in complex formal measures that were praised by the "new critics" and the academic community, were opposed by a vigorous, nonacademic group of poets who valued experience as experience, not as symbol, and who developed a free-form, breath-conditioned verse in accordance with Charles Olson's principles. These poets were first published by such little magazines as *Origin* and the *Black Mountain Review* and by such publishers as Jargon Books (Jonathan Williams) in North Carolina and the Divers Press (Robert Creeley) in Mallorca. They corresponded with one another and gradually extended their influence, became a movement, and affected the practice not only of such beat-generation poets as Allen Ginsberg but also that of a great many other poets, so that by the middle of the 1960's free-form poetry represented the "main stream." Important books of the projective-verse movement include *The Maximus Poems*, by Charles Olson; *The Opening of the Field*, by Robert Duncan; *Here and Now*, by Denise Levertov; and *For Love, Poems 1950–1960*, by Robert Creeley.

The anti-symbolist views of the projective-verse poets were part of a general drift in the late 1950's toward autobiography and family history. This movement represented a rejection of the mythological, archetypal poetry of the early years of the decade. Representative works of the new confessional and autobiographical mode were *Life Studies,* by Robert Lowell, and *Heart's Needle,* by W. D. Snodgrass.

In the late 1950's and early 1960's, Robert Bly and Robert Kelly moved American poetry toward explorations of the subjective world. Dissatisfied with the bareness of much contemporary verse and with the prosaic quality of much coffeehouse poetry, they emphasized imagery that works in a wide register and engages the poet and his reader profoundly. But they evidently had no quarrel with the free forms of projective verse, or with the breath-conditioned line, and so their poems took shape on the page very much in the manner of Creeley, Duncan, and Levertov. James Wright and Louis Simpson found the principles of the movement congenial and made dramatic changes of style that enabled them to write brilliant new poems. Among the important books of this movement are *The Branch Will Not Break,* by James Wright, and *Silence in the Snowy Fields,* by Robert Bly.

Many of these poets express liberal or conservative sentiments, but none of them is committed to a political program in the fashion of the 1930's; none of them writes "kinetic" poetry intended to persuade the reader to a given course of action. There is nothing to correspond to the work of the "angry young men" in England, not even among the beat-generation poets, who express fear of the Bomb and reject the values of "square" society. This does not mean that they are indifferent to the ills of the world; it means, simply, that they respond to instances of illness in a highly personal way. One can see this in the work of the Negro poet LeRoi Jones, who is moved by racial injustice, exposes it, but is wary of slogans.

One can make three complaints about recent American poetry. First of all, many poets under the influence of William Carlos Williams, Louis Zukofsky, and other Objectivists put so much stress on objects, on the "reification" of poetry, that they neglect people, the creation of character. One would like to find a larger population in contemporary poetry. Secondly, in their reaction against the metaphysical subtleties of the symbolist poets, many recent poets have achieved a new dissociation of sensibility that involves a rejection of the intellect in favor of bodily and emotional processes that represent only a part of the life of man. And, thirdly, many of the poets are indifferent to incident, action, plot—which can help to create life in a poem and give it urgency. A poem can be built of a series of perceptions, to be sure, but action is necessary for the best development of character, meaning, and emotion.

Nevertheless, despite these strictures, one can say that reading contemporary poetry is always an exciting experience, for it offers images of the life one knows, and in the idiom of one's own time: one can see the hand of eternity working in the materials of the present. As for the great struggle over prosody—one can find excellent poems in the books of a traditionalist like Richard Wilbur as well as in the books of such innovators as Denise Levertov and James Wright. However, there is no doubt that the poets who have been working in the new free forms have been more successful than their traditionalist colleagues in bringing American poetry close to the breath, voice, and pulse of contemporary life.

SELECTED BIBLIOGRAPHY

Ashbery, John. *Turandot and Other Poems* (1953); *Some Trees* (1956); *The Poems* (1960); *The Tennis Court Oath* (1962).

Bishop, Elizabeth. *North and South* (1946); *Poems* (1955).

Bly, Robert. *Silence in the Snowy Fields* (1962).

Creeley, Robert. *Le Fou* (1952); *The Immoral Proposition* (1953); *The Kind of Act of* (1953); *All That Is Lovely in Men* (1955); *If You* (1956); *The Whip* (1957); *A Form of Women* (1959); *For Love, Poems 1950–1960* (1962).

Dickey, James. *Into the Stone,* in vol. 7, *Poets of Today* (1960); *Drowning With Others* (1962); *Helmets* (1964).

Dugan, Alan. *Poems* (1961); *Poems 2* (1963).

211

Duncan, Robert. *Heavenly City, Earthly City* (1947); *Poems, 1948–1949* (c. 1949); *Medieval Scenes* (1950); *Song of the Borderguard* (1952); *Fragments of a Disordered Devotion* (1952); *Caesar's Gate* (1955); *Letters* (1958); *Selected Poems* (1959); *The Opening of the Field* (1960); *Roots and Branches* (1964).

Garrigue, Jean. *Thirty-Six Poems and a Few Songs,* in *Five Young American Poets,* Third Series (1944); *The Ego and the Centaur* (1947); *The Monument Rose* (1953); *A Water Walk by Villa d'Este* (1959); *Country Without Maps* (1964).

Ginsberg, Allen. *Howl and Other Poems* (1956); *Kaddish and Other Poems: 1958–1960* (1961); *Empty Mirror: Early Poems* (1961); *Reality Sandwiches* (1963).

Jarrell, Randall. *Five Young American Poets,* First Series (1940); *Blood for a Stranger* (1942); *Little Friend, Little Friend* (1945); *Losses* (1948); *The Seven-League Crutches* (1951); *Selected Poems* (1955); *The Woman at the Washington Zoo* (1960); *The Lost World* (1965).

Jones, LeRoi. *Preface to a Twenty Volume Suicide Note* (1961); *The Dead Lecturer* (1964).

Levertov, Denise. *The Double Image* (1946); *Here and Now* (1957); *Overland to the Islands* (1958); *With Eyes at the Back of Our Heads* (1960); *The Jacob's Ladder* (1961); *O Taste and See* (1964).

Lowell, Robert. *Land of Unlikeness* (1944); *Lord Weary's Castle* (1946); *The Mills of the Kavanaughs* (1951); *Life Studies* (1959); *Imitations* (1962); *For the Union Dead* (1964).

Merwin, W. S. *A Mask for Janus* (1952); *The Dancing*

Bears (1954); *Green With Beasts* (1956); *The Drunk in the Furnace* (1960); *The Moving Target* (1963).

Olson, Charles. *Y & X* (1948); *Letter for Melville 1951* (1951); *This* (1952); *The Maximus Poems 1–10* (1953); *Anecdotes of the Late War* (1955); *The Maximus Poems 11–22* (1956); *O'Ryan 246810* (1958); *The Maximus Poems* (1960); *The Distances* (1960); *Maximus, from Dogtown—I* (1961).

Shapiro, Karl. *Poems* (1935); *Five Young American Poets, Second Series* (1941); *Person, Place, and Thing* (1942); *V-Letter and Other Poems* (1944); *Essay on Rime* (1945); *Trial of a Poet* (1947); *Poems, 1940–1953* (1953); *Poems of a Jew* (1958); *The Bourgeois Poet* (1964).

Simpson, Louis. *The Arrivistes* (1949); *Good News of Death* (1955); *A Dream of Governors* (1959); *At the End of the Open Road* (1963).

Stafford, William. *West of Your City* (1960); *Traveling Through the Dark* (1962).

Swenson, May. *Another Animal*, in vol. 1, *Poets of Today* (1954); *A Cage of Spines* (1958); *To Mix with Time: New and Selected Poems* (1963).

Wilbur, Richard. *The Beautiful Changes* (1947); *Ceremony* (1950); *Things of This World* (1956); *Advice to a Prophet* (1961).

Wright, James. *The Green Wall* (1957); *Saint Judas* (1959); *The Branch Will Not Break* (1963).

INDEX

Ashbery, John, 135, 188–190
Auden, W. H., 13, 38, 41, 63, 69

Beat poets, 166–169
Bishop, Elizabeth, 69–79
Blackburn, Paul, 125, 132
Bly, Robert, 16, 119, 175, 176, 179,
  180, 185–187, 208

Confessional poetry, 4, 30, 31, 34
Corso, Gregory, 168, 169
Crane, Hart, 12, 32, 205
Creeley, Robert, 2, 5, 15, 125, 132,
  136, 151–157, 177, 208
Cummings, E. E., 12, 129, 205

Dickey, James, 190–192
Dugan, Alan, 193–194
Duncan, Robert, 15, 125, 132, 136,
  145–151, 157, 177, 208

Eberhart, Richard, 14, 182
Eliot, T. S., 4, 8, 11, 12, 18, 19, 21,
  35, 39, 55, 67, 110, 131, 179, 205

Fearing, Kenneth, 5, 13
Ferlinghetti, Lawrence, 132, 168
Frost, Robert, 8, 9, 49, 50, 127, 182,
  201, 205

Garrigue, Jean, 6, 80–92, 128
Ginsberg, Allen, 133, 166–174, 207

Imagism, 9, 10, 175, 179

Jarrell, Randall, 15, 37–52
Joans, Ted, 132, 168
Jones, LeRoi, 195–198, 209

Kelly, Robert, 175, 176, 177, 178,
  179, 180, 208

Kerouac, Jack, 6, 135, 166, 168

Levertov, Denise, 15, 125, 132, 136, 157–165, 177, 208, 210
Lowell, Robert, 5, 15, 17–36, 37, 40, 49, 118, 128, 208

Masters, Edgar Lee, 8, 10
Melville, Herman, 25, 35, 137, 138, 142
Merwin, W. S., 6, 15, 107–123
Moore, Marianne, 12, 49, 54, 64, 70, 205

New criticism, 15, 18, 31, 116, 124, 207

Olson, Charles, 15, 119, 125, 126, 128, 129, 130, 132, 136–145, 157, 160, 169, 175, 183, 207

Pejorocracy, 137, 140, 142, 144
Pound, Ezra, 8, 10, 11, 12, 67, 108, 125, 126, 128, 131, 140, 141, 179, 205
Projective verse, 15, 116, 128, 129, 130, 136, 150, 151, 157, 158, 169, 177, 180, 189, 196, 208

Ransom, John Crowe, 5, 13, 15, 18, 22, 49, 124
Robinson, Edwin Arlington, 8, 9, 182

Rothenberg, Jerome, 175, 177
Rukeyser, Muriel, 13, 14

Sandburg, Carl, 10, 11
Seidel, Frederick, 30, 31
Sexton, Anne, 5, 15
Shapiro, Karl, 14, 53–68
Simpson, Louis, 198–200, 208
Snodgrass, W. D., 5, 15, 118, 128, 208
Stafford, William, 201–202
Stevens, Wallace, 4, 8, 10, 11, 12, 49, 148, 164, 189
Subjective imagery, 16, 119, 175–187, 199
Swenson, May, 6, 202–204

Tate, Allen, 13, 18, 19, 22

Warren, Robert Penn, 13, 15
Whitman, Walt, 4, 6, 9, 49, 67, 119, 125, 135, 170, 174, 199
Wilbur, Richard, 15, 93–106, 128, 210
Williams, William Carlos, 2, 10, 12, 17, 49, 67, 70, 125, 128, 131, 140, 205, 209
Wright, James, 16, 119, 175, 180–185, 208, 210

Yeats, William Butler, 11, 67, 81